To The Sharmas family

May your Days Be full of Light always.

Monique Douskas

From Ghetto
to Glory

# From Ghetto to Glory

## A Memoir

### Monique Douglass-Andrews

HAMPTON ROADS
PUBLISHING COMPANY, INC.
for the evolving human spirit

Cover design by Jane Hagaman
Cover art by Anne L. Louque

Hampton Roads Publishing Company, Inc.
1125 Stoney Ridge Road
Charlottesville, VA 22902

434-296-2772
fax: 434-296-5096
e-mail: hrpc@hrpub.com
www.hrpub.com

If you are unable to order this book from your local
bookseller, you may order directly from the publisher.
Call 1-800-766-8009, toll-free.

Library of Congress Cataloging-in-Publication Data

Andrews, Monique, 1969-
From ghetto to glory : a memoir / Monique Andrews.
    p. cm.
ISBN 1-57174-368-5 (acid-free paper)
1. Andrews, Monique, 1969- 2. Multiple personality--Patients--United
States--Biography. 3. African American women--Biography. I. Title.
  RC569.5.M8 A53 2002
  616.85'236'0092--dc21
                                    2002011721

ISBN 1-57174-368-5
10 9 8 7 6 5 4 3 2 1
Printed on acid-free paper in Canada

While this story is true, names have been changed to protect the innocent.

# *One*

Hi. My name is Sookie. It's not Silky or Cookie, just Sookie. That's what my daddy named me. I am the youngest of four and the only girl. Can't nobody tell me nothing about my brothers that I don't already know. These guys taught me how to spit, fight, climb trees, and steal soda from the soda pop man. They all were my daddies. I considered myself lucky after Daddy left 'cause now I had three daddies. I also knew they weren't going anywhere no time soon, 'specially if Mama kept cooking the way she always did.

Of course, out of my three daddies, one was around more than the others. But that's just because he was the youngest of the three, and Mama could never find the other two. I called him Daddy Bubba. He always had the duty of looking after me while Mama was in nursing school studying to be a registered nurse. He took me everywhere possible, 'cept when he snuck out the window to see that ol' stank girl, Ginny. There's no other way to 'scribe this girl. She smelled like old fish and was plain. She was white, too, and not even a model kind of pretty.

After Daddy left Mama for a white lady, I learned all kinds of names for that race of people. Mama would just sit on the front porch, and the soft orange-yellow light from the bug bulb would hit the shackles of our house, and then touch her black hair lightly, causing her hair to shimmer. It would shimmer like the waves on the surface of a river. It was warm that night as I sat beside her. She cried her eyes out under the stars. She was beautiful. She was in pain. She'd ask herself questions like, what did he see in that hussy, that cow? The whole thing just busted her wide open with hurt.

I guess Daddy Bubba was just testing the waters out, trying to see what my biological daddy was getting from this woman he left my mama for. In a way, my daddy brothers all had a special love for each other, 'cause they kinda shared ol' Ginny, just at different times, you know. Maybe, that's why she smelled so. Each of them would take their turns lifting up the window to their room they shared near the back of the upstairs.

Looks like it was once an enclosed porch, where someone would sit and let the sun bounce off of 'em. It was so narrow and thin in their room. Seems like they always chose the middle window, too, seein' that the roof being so weak with wood gutters an' all, landing in the center of it just made more sense. Once they climbed out the window, they would then let their legs dangle until the tips of their toes hit the bottom half of the back porch. Suddenly they were on the ground and running through our metal gate. Ol' Ginny sure better be where she was 'posed to be!

Anyway, Daddy Bubba, no matter where his night ventures took him, was always back by morning. And we were off on his dirt bike to have free lunch in Irving Park under the Reading Tree. I loved the Reading Tree. I loved going to Irving Park with him, even though folks say it used to be an ol' graveyard; that's why it was so hilly and why kids were always getting into fights and things there. Daddy Bubba always gave me his cookie from those free lunches, too. He'd reach onto his plate and hand me his soft chewy chocolate chip cookie. I guess it made it easier for him to run off and swing from those monkey bars. I believe he broke his right arm a total of five times between the monkey bars and climbing trees. Thank God, he was left-handed.

Growing up with three daddies wasn't that bad. The other two, I got to see them when they weren't running the streets, pretending to be pimps in the daytime and gentlemen by night. They were just trying their best to impress those sweet church girls they dated.

It seems, too, we had a night each month when Mama must've gotten a good share of tips from her night job. She would let me go to the Alberta Street Theater with my daddy brothers. This theater had white cement walls, and old, red velvet chairs. The movie screen would kinda drop down in the center of what seemed to have been a stage for live performances. After the end of the movies, kids would run up onto the platform and dance, make bunny ears, and let their shadows bounce from behind the screen. The owner never got angry, though; it's almost as if he expected it. We'd usually see Bruce Lee flicks. My favorite one was *Enter the Dragon*.

It would be me, Daddy Bubba, Daddy Tee, and Daddy Chaz, all struttin' to that broken down ol' theater. We'd put our feet up on those velvet seats, just in case a rat decided to trot by and help himself to some stale popcorn. My favorite part of going to the movies, though, was coming home. Each of us got to be someone from the movie. We'd punch and kick walls; we'd even kick each other all the way home.

Once we got home, we'd make spaghetti noodles with no sauce in Mama's pink flamingo-colored kitchen and pretend to eat like the folks in the picture show. After we were done, we'd hold hands and form a semicircle. One brother would hold the handle of the cast-iron pot. I'd be in the middle, and another brother would be on the other end counting to three before he put his hand on the handle of the white refrigerator. The light electrical shock would make us all jump and then giggle profusely.

On those evenings, I don't believe anybody snuck out the window to see ol' Ginny. It would be me and my daddy brothers, laughing with shock and speaking Chinese all night long.

*So you ask yourself who I am? Well, I'll tell you who I am. I'm that little voice inside Sookie's head that keeps her going. Yup, those times when she's telling the story and she feel like she 'bout to fall off the face of the Earth, 'bout to die inside 'cause the truth hurt so bad . . . I come and help her on, give her a break in the telling.*

*Oh, I know folk don't want to admit they got little voices in their head, but it's true, that small, still voice that tells you to move on, or that loud voice that tells you to go ahead, shoot yourself. Well, I am the soft voice, that's what's needed here, a soft voice to come in, pick up the pace, encourage— shoot, even bring a smile if I can.*

*Don't tell Sookie you know, but there were times when Sookie was writing this story and she just stop, right in the middle of a sentence, and cry 'till her eyes were swollen. There were times when she was writing and threw her pen and book against the wall. 'Cause, see, Sookie didn't trust them computer things at all, thought she'd work her way through a bloody scene, and the thing would blow up, lose everything she had done made herself remember, so she did everything by longhand. Sometimes she'd jump up, and nobody'd know where she going, and she'd drive, very hard and very fast, until I come and have her to remember there are folk back home who really do love her, tell her don't do it, Sookie . . . you got's to go on.*

*Well, that's what I do. Call me an angel, or a part of her conscience, or whatever works for you, as long as it ain't no demon or devil, 'cause I'm not that kinda voice. Just know that it was me who'd whisper ever so gently in her ear and pull her heart up, causing her to wipe her face and go on.*

*But that's kinda personal, so just tuck that info away, okay? Anyway, just don't worry too much about me. Just keep on with the reading and you'll see for yourself just how Sookie make it through this little shop of horror.*

*Now, every time Sookie goes to share this story, something don't rest right inside her unless she tries to tell about the house, what she and her daddy brothers now refer to as "that" house. Seems as though each of us distanced ourselves from it in our own way. It now seems like it was haunted.*

The house was goldish tan, rippled on the outside like a ruffled potato chip. It was a big house, with six bedrooms.

One room, nobody could go in because nothing seemed to stay alive in it. It was made of cement and always cold. Mama called it the coal room. She said it was where they kept the coal to heat the house. The house was built in 1907, which makes it almost a hundred years old. Mama said they used to lift up the window, now bound with wood, and the coal would be poured directly in from the outside.

This room was in the basement. The coal marks still frantically sketch the walls. They're scattered around like signs of a struggle. The inside of the door is charred and burned from so much heat being locked in there. On the doorknob, all around it, there were always these small finger and handprints, as if some little person tried to get out but couldn't. Defeated and tired, they'd lay against those cold, cement walls and be consumed by the discomfort, the closeness of the area, the coal fumes, and the light smell of gas. They were consumed by the fact that no matter how high or how much they yelled, beyond that heavy wood door, which at one time was a clear, sky blue, they couldn't be heard.

Beyond the furnace, just outside the door, with the noise of the fire, no one would ever hear them. Although this room stayed empty, the walls seemed to breathe after Daddy left. They would go in and out slowly, like a pair of lungs. But it would only do this when Mama wasn't home. It seems as if whatever was alive down in this coal room traveled through the walls, making the whole house come alive. That's why the house is so unique. At times, the walls would stop breathing, and they'd sweat instead. I began to get worried, and started to think Mama should stay home at night, but how would I get those new tenny-shoe skates? How would my brothers get their new clothes?

One night on the way upstairs, I almost touched those walls. Instead, I ran. Daddy had been gone awhile now, and ugly was startin' to creep all through the house. I began to see more things, imagine more, 'cause it took me out of those walls—that eventually began to bleed.

*Stay with me now, 'cause I think it's beyond grace and mercy how God gets the victory out of this story, and I want to tell it straight. Besides, she saw something that hit the nail on the head. It was a sticker that said, "If the devil tries to remind you of your past, remind him of his future." That's what she's going to do. Now, she ain't no Stephen King, but ugly hides everywhere, and I tell you, ugly was in them bleeding walls. She used to wonder why did these things only happen when Mama was gone. Come to find out, Mama saw things in that house, too.*

See, Mama had been sittin' on our green sofa chairs that rested on them reflection-clean hardwood floors. She was tired. She worked two jobs and had done went to school that day, too. She said she sensed something, so she turned around and coming up from the basement stairs she saw a middle-aged lady; she was white. She had a nineteenth-century high hat on and a scarf around her neck, along with a white gown.

Mama just watched her as she turned and passed through our living room wall, which encased a peephole that would allow you to see from the steps, directly into the living room. Why did that house have so many peepholes? Anyway, this ghost lady kept going, then went right up the wooden steps. I wonder if every fourth one creaked as it did to me the many times I went up and down them, when me and Daddy Bubba tried to see Santa Claus.

Mama said she got up, kinda shook her head and rose to walk around. As she walked through the rooms, she was yellin', "I don't know who you are, or what you want, but you bed' not touch my chillun'!" She then just went on to get her rest. She said we were all out playing that day, our chores had been done and we were free.

I believe it's 'cause ugly can sense a woman of God. It don't want to be nowhere 'round something Godly. It just goes back down there to hell, which I believe is where that coal room led to, and waits for an opportunity to come back again. Ugly gets in folks too—anybody. It crawled right into my daddy brothers, tried to steal them right away from me. But see, God was watching the whole time. He saw me lose one daddy—sho' 'nough wasn't gonna let me lose three.

*There's no easy way to tell about this ugly, either. She can't sugarcoat this story for you. Just stay with her and hold her hand during the tellin'.*

It started when I was six. My imagination has always been real active; at least that's what my mama say. She'd say, "Sookie, you can think up anything." Sometimes, she'd even have me tell stories to her sick patients. But my imagination was always the key to my soul. She just didn't know. Mama didn't know.

I didn't have a lot of friends when my family and I moved to Oregon from Washington, D.C. in 1975. I just spent a whole lot of time with my dolls. Baby Alive, Barbie, Ken, and the gang. But my favorite possession was my dollhouse. It was metal and Mama stayed up all night long to put it together. She painted all the little people a beautiful brown. That was the thing in the seventies, identifying with your culture, by any means necessary. All the figurines were starting to peel and look albino, but it was all right by me. Mama took the time to detail them, so I could play with a family that looked like ours. She set them out in front of their painted metal lawn under the Christmas tree. It was perfect, really. It was kind of symbolic, 'cause dad was still living with us at the time.

The dollhouse had two floors for me to decorate all by myself. When Daddy Bubba was not looking, I'd snag one of his favorite matchbox cars for the family to ride on top of. I made sure to get the cars with doors that would open; those were always the best.

That Christmas was a good one. Everybody seemed to have gotten what they wanted. Daddy Tee got his science set. He was always trying out experimental things, being that Daddy was a doctor an' all. He wanted to be like him. He did amazing things with that science set, too, like set beds on fire, and set the attic on fire, and burn holes on our wooden floors as he tried endlessly to find his contact lenses in the midst of his own smoke.

Daddy Chaz finally got his drum set. It was blue and sparkled like the frost on the outside of an ice-cream box. Daddy took all night to put that together, too. Mama said he was cussing at the drum set and she would just tell him, "It'll be over soon." The smile on Daddy Chaz's face come morning time made Daddy's heart smile. He knew then, yeah, it was worth it. Daddy Bubba got his banana boat skateboard. It was yellow, narrow, and perfect for his daring feet. I snuck it to school one day. I fell, too, all the way down what we called Sabin Hill and I broke my right arm. I guess it was only for him. The pogo sticks were for us all though! We headed to the driveway and jumped, and jumped, and jumped, until we reached the beginning of blue in the sky. We were rich. We had Mama and Daddy, and we were all in love.

When Daddy was home, things seemed so complete. In the spring, he'd come home from naturopathic school and sneak up behind Mama in the kitchen. He'd tell her to stop what she was doing, which would be frying chicken, cooking spaghetti, or making lentils and rice. He'd tell her we were leaving for the weekend, so she'd better round us all up. Mama would pack that wooden picnic basket so tight the aromas would seep through the cracks. We'd all pile into the brown Dodge van and the six of us would be off, just like that. Daddy didn't call from his school to warn Mama, he'd just show up as if all his labs and studying finally took their toll on him. And it was just time, plain and simple, time to love us all.

Me and Mom stuck together on those trips with three brothers and a spontaneous dad on the loose; we had to. They had a great time, my dad and my brothers, fishing. Daddy loved his fishing pole; it came 3,000 miles from the East Coast. It was so historical that he took to hiding it after our ventures, so my brothers couldn't get to it. He always looked so much taller with his fishing pole, at home, happy. On these trips my dad and brothers would also throw rocks and go hiking. But the all-time get up on those nights was Dad releasing all that built-up stress on his congas. In the middle of the woods, we'd bounce around and Mom would regurgitate her ol' African dances and have a showdown in front of Daddy. The world then became just the two of them. Me and my brothers would become invisible, meshed in with the grass, trees, sky, and stars. If ever they made love, they made it on nights like those.

*You know, ever since Sookie's been trying to tell this story, now going on five years, it seems like a part of her gets really crazy inside. It's like she's walking around crying out, but no one can hear her. And it's no subtle cry, but a loud scream. Because each time another day goes by, a part of her seems to close up and almost die, fearing that she's another step closer to not telling this story.*

*She tries to reassure that ol' broken down part of her, everything is going to be okay. She tries to say that this time God's timing seems to be no less than perfect. But that part, that voice in her, just keeps hollerin' and so she's asking you all to stick with her on the tellin' part. Stick with her, or else she's sure to go deaf from so much of her own self-hollerin'.*

*Mama and Daddy were perfect in her eyesight. Her family had what most kids on her block didn't have, a daddy.*

*That's probably why she loved the dollhouse so. She controlled the coming and going of all the family members. She controlled the way the house looked. It was her, Sookie, who controlled when they ate, played, and slept. It was never like when her daddy really left her, and she could make sure it would never be like that. And I guess that's why the dollhouse was her favorite.*

See, Daddy left Mama in a hurry that summer. Mama was in the dining room. I could hear their voices from the back porch. Mama began at first by talking to him, asking him questions, then her voice slowly began to rise and rise, until the windows began to shake with her anger. Daddy was quiet. He didn't have much to say because that's how guilt works. He knew he did wrong, and when it came time to say something, his voice just disappeared, like I tried to do when I entered the house and heard the two of them.

Mama, then, began walking around the wooden dining room table. The prayer plant rested in the middle of it. It came all the way from Washington D.C., just to die as she threw it against the built-in china cabinet, busting the glass windows. The clay pot busted and Daddy sat down in the living room, eyes wide. Mama didn't cry right away. It wasn't until it was silent that I could hear her tears as Daddy took some clothes and left. She wanted him to hurry and leave.

But it wasn't that simple and pinpointed. Daddy had done wrong. He lost his mind when Mama went back to D.C. to see her grandmamma buried.

She left the four of us with him in Oregon. Why shouldn't she? He was, after all, our father. But while Mama was having her tears evaporate in the hot, sticky, summer sun back east, Daddy was burning things up at home with some woman my daddy brothers said he met in a strip joint. I took their word on the woman's career, 'cause the eldest two were always sneaking into some place, trying to be men.

This woman, though, she was nothing like Mama. She was white, which was a no-no, 'specially in the 70s when we were pro-black, pro-afro, pro-cornrows, pro-chitlins and greens. So, that put her in a class of her own. She was immediately our enemy, 'cause she was not one of us.

Dad was kooky enough to introduce us to her, too. Yeah, he told us all we were going to spend the day together on the Willamette River, fishing in our boat. Yeah, the boat he bought for the six of us. Note, the six of us. Anyway, when we got out of the van to unhitch the boat, we decided together to torture her, and ask her all sorts of questions, while the crabs ran in front of us. She had no business in my mama's front seat, anyway.

This woman looked about twenty, which confirmed my daddy brothers sayin' how Dad must've been in his mid-life crisis. They didn't seem mad at all, at least not then. I just kept checking this lady out. I was thinking the whole time, "Is this woman trying to steal my daddy from my mama? My beautiful mama." Man, I don't care how you tried to paint this woman like my dolls were, she'd never have been pretty as my mama, my beautiful brown mama. But whatever she had, it was good enough for Daddy to leave the five of us.

In a new place and an old house where spirits lived and eventually began to live in us, we became their prey. See, when Daddy was home, ugly was knocking on the door, but couldn't get in. When Dad left, the door was cracked. Mama could've shut it, but because she was weak, ugly had a chance to get in. She was weak, like down to the ground weak. When Daddy was home, she was always strong. See, there is always something evil out there waiting to get in your heart, but with love and God it has no chance. Daddy and Mama were love. Take love away and close your eyes to God and evil has every chance in hell of getting in and taking over.

*Have you ever known you were supposed to tell a story and tried to run from that truth anyway? Despite what you want to do, it's as if God almost has to conk you on your head so you can get down to the business of tellin'. It's just the way we humans are, I suppose. Somehow, we can fear ourselves and even our deep, dark truths that are, in the end, somehow supposed to bring light. Well, it's darkest before the dawn now, ain't it?*

Daddy's and Mama's paradise faded fast once Mama came back from her grandmamma's funeral. Any woman with some dignity, of which Mama had a lot, would put a cheatin' man out on his back. So when she did, we all cried. That's when I thought white women had some sort of secret power. This is when I also fell in love with Wonder Woman and Dyna Girl.

I started to make friends some. Friends are one thing that don't come often, not like the ones I had. Emma and Tasha blended right into the times. But I never played with them, just the three of us; it was always one or the other. See, Tasha was from the part of the neighborhood where there were a lot of blacks, and Emma was around my block.

Emma, wow. I loved her. She was a full-blooded Black Foot Indian. She, to me, was like banana pudding, something Mama only made every once in awhile. But when you ate it, it sure was good and it was a taste you could remember for days on top of days. We always had a good time. We didn't have to go far from our neighborhood to have an adventure.

See, she was a couple of years younger than me, but we both came from secret prisons. And although it was years before we found this out about each other, we just loved each other through it all, through the secrets. We took pleasure in the same crazy games, in roller skating around her basement for hours at a time, jumping off the workmen's countertops down there; we were stunt girls! We'd make up names for our stunts on skates, too. We'd name our moves after wrestlers, like Jay Youngblood and Joe Lightfoot. They were the best! Despite how yucky boys were, I wanted to marry Jay Youngblood. We were half-Indian anyway, right?

No matter how much time lapsed between Emma and me, we could always come back together and pick up where we left off. That was the best thing about her. We were sisters. When my perfect family came tumbling down, she was there.

At times I'd isolate myself, though, and take to the comfort of my pink room. My room was more than pink, though; it was mine! It had mirrors that graced the left side of the wall as you entered it, complete with a ballet bar, so I could practice and practice being a ballerina. I've danced since I was six, a gift from my mama and daddy. I had a Holly Hobby record player that would play the 50 Great Music Treasures: "Blue Danube," "Song of India," "Over the Waves," "Waltz of the Flowers," and "Flight of the Bumble Bee," to name a few.

I was the nightingale in one of my first recitals. Mama sat on the front row as I blossomed from my cage in my glittery-gold bird suit complete with beak. Daddy was down the hall, in his lab, watching tubes of blood shake 'round and 'round.

My classes were in the same building he worked in. He'd rush home in the middle of the day to take me to class. I'd change in the back of the van as he sped to get us back downtown. When my class was over, it would be the end of his workday, too. He'd then take me to the nature store across the street and buy me a sesame seed cracker, drizzled with honey for a nickel. I know he peeked in the window that day as I danced for him, for Mama, for us to never end.

My daddy brothers began to get wilder. Dad was gone. Mama was working and going to school, plus my daddy brothers were angry, and wildness plus anger don't mix too well. With a little time, those two things can do something to young minds. Daddy Tee, the eldest, pimped. Maybe he thought he could justify things somehow, by becoming a Mac daddy and having women bring him money, in exchange for selling their bodies.

He loved money, quick money. He didn't like money that came once a month, or every two weeks, for that matter. He had lots of stuff, like Cadillacs. I liked going to his apartment once he moved out, 'cause then I could go through his hookers' things.

He beat these girls sometimes. Anger can come out like that. I guess a pimp was the farthest thing from what my daddy was. Nobody wanted to be like him anymore. So the race was on for all of us to establish our own identity, somehow, someway. I loved Daddy Tee for being the first one to step out and do this, to be his own person. He did it in a way the whole neighborhood could see, so nobody messed with him, or us.

Daddy Bubba just laughed. He was busy making others laugh, too, and he had a lot of friends. I only had two, but he had a whole nation. I figured this was just his way; the more laughter, the less pain. Mama spent enough time crying, and as her son, he was going to do his darndest to bring her some internal sunshine. He gave a lot, too, more than just cookies from the park lunches. He went as far as to seek out churches, where they had cool things like candy rains. The Sunday school teachers would climb on top of the church roof, and throw candy down at all the kids. What I couldn't catch in my dress, Daddy Bubba would make up for, by giving me some of his.

He would also take me to this church off Albina Street. There, if you sat through the Sunday school class and church, you could pick packs and packs of free cookies. I loved the soft, chewy oatmeal and raisin ones, and the ones lightly touched with icing that had a hint of molasses in them.

You'll notice I talk about Daddy Bubba more, not because I love him more than my other brothers, but because he really was internal sunshine, and you tend to remember things like that in the midst of the storm. Of course, during our growing up all my daddy brothers had an everlasting impact on me, one more so than the others. I never knew I could harbor secrets the way I began to after my dad left. I owe that talent to Daddy Chaz.

*Daddy Chaz. He's a sentence all by himself. He don't need nothin' but a period after his name. But Sookie, she got to tell the rest anyway. She has to fill you in, give you the commas and things. Daddy Chaz is the middle brother. He, unlike Daddy Tee, didn't take to the boldness of being a ladies' man in an outlandish sort of way. Instead, he took to crime. He was extremely in love with Dad, and by him leaving, Daddy Chaz was beyond anger.*

Now that I'm older, I realize Daddy Chaz was just aching like the rest of us when he went out and stole things or hit neighbors' kids over their heads with crowbars. I finally realized it was the pain of being left that drove him to find revenge in my innocence.

There I said it. He took my innocence; he molested me. And the walls of that house began to move and bleed more. He soon was going back and forth between juvy and home. So, between his comings and goings, he made sure to threaten me. He said he'd kill my mama and my long-gone daddy if I ever told. So, I kept ever so quiet. Little did I know, my dollhouse would not be enough to hide behind. My dolls would not be enough to hide behind. My closet would not be enough. My pink room, not enough. Nothing would be enough. And my dear sweet mama, beneath my smiles, beneath my dancing feet, she never knew. Mama never knew.

*Mama never knew, not until later and it's too soon to tell that part, so you all are gonna have to wait for that. There is still a lot of growing parts that still need to be told. Now, aren't you glad I'm here? Sookie, she keep coming and going. I guess she needs a break from the tellin' part of this. It's not an easy thing. But it wouldn't be right if I didn't let you all into her mind some, her insanity that come from this Daddy Chaz. Can you believe he crept into her dreams? Sho' 'nough, snuck right into her subconscious.*

*Sookie, she try to cope. She was only six, seven, eight, nine, and then ten! She loved that pink room her mama painted for her. She would try to disappear into her closet walls, like the kids did in* The Lion, The Witch and The Wardrobe. *But she'd just come straight into contact with them bleeding walls. She tried to play dolls. She tried to build tents, using her mama's chairs. She tried to be invisible, and she even tried crawling out onto the roof.*

*But I believe ugly loves innocence and innocent children. This ugly would just walk around her house. Nights were the worst for Sookie, see, 'cause her mama was gone. This ugly pranced around the living room, the dinette, kitchen, and TV room. But I myself believed it lived in the basement. It probably swam 'round in that empty cement room. The coal room that no one could stay in, 'cause they'd probably freeze to death in there. Funny though, I thought hell was supposed to be hot. If Mama did know, she probably would've killed it. That is probably why it never went in the storage room, where the extra food was kept, too much good stuff that Mama would put her hands on to cook with. Ugly fears good. And if Mama had the slightest idea that ugly was walking around the house, after she done kissed her baby girl goodnight, I bet some more prayer plants would've went flying.*

When Daddy Chaz was gone from home was when I started seeing ghosts in that house. They were always so old looking. There were always two, they were female, and one was shorter than the other. The shorter one looked like a child, just used up, is all. It was like she wanted to tell me something, but her tongue would never move. Mine wouldn't move either when I saw the two of them, swinging from the corner of the right side of the wall on my white dresser edge. My tongue would never let me scream. After watching me awhile, they'd just disappear into what seemed like nowhere, but was actually everywhere around me.

One day Daddy Chaz happened to be home. It was the Fourth of July weekend. I had played in my closet as long as possible. I even leaned my ear against the wall, and it seemed as if I could hear a thousand voices. They were not Mama's or any of my daddy brothers, but other folks, children. Some were crying; some were whispering. I think these walls were protecting me, 'cause Daddy Chaz never came into the closet.

One time I heard him tell Mama he woke up in the middle of the night and he saw the devil standin' at the foot of his bed, chains and all. She didn't laugh, nor did she smile. She just listened carefully, trying to analyze what it was her son was truly trying to say. I believed him. In my opinion, it was probably one of the ghost people, dressed up, trying to scare him off so he couldn't come near me, the bastard.

Yeah, I know; how can I call a brother of mine a bastard when we come from the same mother? How? You know, people go crazy in their own way. They do so to cope with the issues that are trying to engulf them like hot flames. It seems he'd gone crazy. And by age ten I began to slowly drift away, not understanding my dad's departure, and Daddy Chaz, who could've been a pimp instead of messing with me, making me feel like the dirty girl.

Daddy Bubba still looked over me, but as I said, I began to do different things; nobody or nothing was enough. It was around this time that I met a new girl. Emma was still cool to me, but there was something about this girl that took me out of my world of closets, ghosts, and confused daddy brothers. Her name was Jasmine. Jasmine was a tall, lanky black girl and an only child. Her father was a full-blown alcoholic, and her mom, mean as the Wicked Witch in *The Wiz*. She had a Doberman pinscher who always barked, even if he couldn't see you. We used to steal cookies out of her mother's kitchen, and then eat them in her room. She had a canopy bed just like mine, and lots of toys just like me. I guess being an only child is a lot like being the only girl.

But whenever her dad came home, I left in a hurry. I'd watch Jasmine turn from a smiling brown doll to a nervous pickaninny. It was as if she had two faces. I almost hated to leave her, but I was, for some reason, terrified of her father and whatever it was that lived in his eyes. I'd run all the way home, usually spotting Daddy Bubba and his friends, who were in some neighbor's backyard with a brown bag hyper-ventilating. He'd let me join in sometimes, only with extreme caution. He loved me, Daddy Bubba; too bad he could not see into me. I kept my secret about Daddy Chaz all too well, saving the life of my mama and far away daddy. Little did I know, the more I held it in, the more the house came alive.

# Two

There was a ghost in the house and her name was Nellie. After Daddy Chaz crept around my insides, I began to see her a lot. Well, I never actually saw her, but I talked to her an awful lot. She wouldn't show herself to me. She always felt I wasn't ready. But she let me know a lot of things about that house. She told me others died in this house. She told me they were murdered and buried in the cement basement and in the walls. I wanted to know why she was telling me all this. She told me because they were young, like me, and they, too, were also hurt by family members in all their special places. I didn't want to hear this. But she said I could save them if I wanted, all I'd have to do is share my body with them, give them a place other than those breathing walls to live in, a place away from their pain.

I wasn't sure about that, but she left me with the power to decide. I guess the spirit that got into those people was still in that house, you know, the spirit that hurt them. I guess it crawled right into Daddy Chaz. Why not? We were all wide open with hurt and pain from Daddy leaving. If I weren't raised better, I'd curse my daddy.

When Mama was up and rested one morning, I went to her in the kitchen she loved so much, where smells of peach cobbler, macaroni and cheese, and chicken dripped from the white metal stove. This was the kitchen we shot peas in, so they'd stick to the ceiling. This was a place where banana puddings were made, and bellies were filled with the black-eyed peas and liver we fed to the six-toed cat named Taurus.

Mama spotted me standing there and smiled. I got the chair I always jumped off of, from my many attempts to try and fly. I decided to sit in it this time, and wait for her listening ear. She looked over at me and I spoke.

"Mama, I have a friend. Her name is Nellie. She told me there are some little girls buried in the walls here, and that I can save them."

Mama looked at me, but kept on cooking, stirring her aromas around the kitchen. Spaghetti, good.

I went on, "Anyway, Mama, haven't you always wondered why weird things happen around here, like when you fold up the linen and put it in the closet, only to come back and find it knocked down?"

She told me, "It's because of the cats."

I told her, "No, it isn't. It's because we have ghosts in here."

Mama kept stirring.

"You know Mama, I could share my body with them, get them out of those walls, free them."

Mama put her wooden spoon down. She told me, "Listen," so I opened my ears. She said, "I know you miss your daddy, but we've got to move on, to pick up and trust God. Besides, it isn't a good thing to share your body with spirits, don't entertain them. A bad one could get in and take over."

I sat still. What? How bad could little girls be? I told her again, "I have a chance to save them."

Mama said sternly, "No." She told me to tell Nellie I can't do it.

I left the kitchen and the smell of garlic behind. This time when I passed the living room walls to go upstairs, I could've sworn I saw them move, but Mama taught us not to swear.

I decided I'd tell Nellie tomorrow. I decided I'd tell her I'd do it. Only because I knew what it felt like to be murdered at such a young age. I wanted to save those girls, free them, even though it was against Mama's will.

You must know at this point in my life, I was too young to

realize I was opening a can of worms. I was too young to realize I was hiding and too young to know I could ever be saved. I wanted to escape. I wanted Narnia, still. I wanted a dollhouse, white picket fences, and my innocence back. But it was too late, I thought. So, I kept going with the flow and created my own little insanity playground. But this insanity kept me alive. *It kept me alive!*

*Memories*. Memories. These are different from dreams. You cannot wake up from them and make them up with your bed in the morning. Sharing my body with the little girls would just make all the memories easier. So I thought.

*Memories*. We had a dog. Her name was Tina. She died under Daddy Chaz's bed and her blood stained the carpet. The bloodstain stayed there.

*I remember now*. The first time was when he called me to his room.

He had been picking his hair with that red-green-and-black-handled afro comb. I remember him saying, "Come here, Mona." Never Sookie, always Mona. I remember my back hitting the carpet where the dog's blood had stained the carpet. It had been a year since Tina had died. I remember screaming, "Stop it! It hurts! Stop it!" Then it was just, "No. No. NO!" He liked it.

White stuff got all over my belly. He was wearing white socks. They were dirty. I remember blackness. I remember awakening being all alone, cold and empty. I remember a lady taking me by the hand leading me to the bathtub. A ghost lady with a white scarf around her neck, and a nineteenth-century high hat on her head. She washed me that day. Mama was at school. Daddy Bubba, gone. Daddy Tee, gone. I hate socks on me. I hate thick white socks. *You can't wash it off! You can't wash it off. . . .*

I loved Nellie for rescuing me.

Daddy Tee finally fell in love with a girl who could sing the heavens open. Her name was Gigi. She was beautiful, too. She was beautiful enough to make my Daddy Tee get a real job and talk about moving up the right way. Mama was okay with that, and Daddy Tee kept bringing money home to help. I suspected Mama would be at Geneva's more now, to try to help finance a wedding, a dream for her eldest son.

Daddy Chaz was in jail now. He outgrew juvy and so did his crimes. So, I was relaxed more when night came. Besides, I had Nellie, Daddy Bubba, and the little girls. Yes, I had let them in, all seven of them. I just opened up my soul and let them all in at once. These girls did not have actual names like me and Emma. But they were called something, all of them. There was Moan, Mona, The Twins, The Mommy Part, Blue, and The Mean Part.

These girls were the sweetest, too, in their own ways. They did the bravest thing ever, too; they promised, *promised* to help save me from Daddy Chaz, since I saved them, freed them from those breathing cement walls. We were a team now.

In the comfort of my room, they came out. Sometimes, I would sit in front of the mirror and a low growl would come from my deepest insides and one would appear. They could never appear without making some sort of nerve-racking sound.

The first time I saw one was when I looked into my mirror that Mama had fixed so nicely, the dresser and mirror set she found at a garage sale. It was good furniture, stuff they don't make anymore. She brought that dresser set home. She sanded it and sanded it with her green and white scarf on. Then, she painted and shellacked it and took us out on a drive so we didn't have to smell the fumes. When we came home, she set it against the right side of the wall, and as you entered the room, your eyes couldn't help but lay gently on it. I guess the little girls liked that mirror, too.

The growl would come, then I'd look close to the mirror and there she was. I reckon this was The Mean Part. She had thick eyebrows, very thick, and her eyes were brown, but her face was stuck into a mean, mean frown. She used to look back at me in the mirror and tell me that she hated me, she hated me! Why? I rescued her. But she did. Sometimes she'd spit onto the mirror or try and scratch it with her fingers. She would pull my hair sometimes and that hurt. She'd pull the ponytails Mama put in my hair. But she never stayed too long, at least not then. She would disappear at the first sign of Mama coming home, or anyone coming up the steps.

Sometimes, Moan would come and visit me in the mirror. But her eyes were always swollen from crying so much. Poor thing. I would look at her and tell her not to cry, that Mama would be home soon, but she never seemed to listen, just kept drippin' all over the mirror! I pushed her once, back in. I did not want to clean up her stinky tears. Why was she always so sad anyway? I rescued her.

My favorite one to see was The Mommy Part. She was different. You could never really tell what she was going to do next. We would talk. She'd come to the mirror and her growl, before she appeared, was never as ugly sounding as the others' were. We'd talk about dolls and how pretty the light pink room was. She loved the ballet bars. She loved the closet, too. She couldn't go in there though, only me.

One time, Mama gave me some leftover homemade dough from one of her peach cobblers. I sat there at the mirror with a doll named Toby. I let The Mommy Part peek in on me feeding him.

She smiled at that. She told me that day that among all the other ones, all the other little girls, she would be the one always there for me. I kissed her that day, leaving my mouth print on the mirror. I will never forget that day, that kiss.

Mama came home that day with Lillian, a crystal white New Zealand Rabbit. She had the pinkest eyes ever! She matched perfectly with my room and she was real. The Mommy Part disappeared when she heard Mama's Volkswagen come up the driveway.

I rose to meet Mama down the hall as she called me. There Lillian was. She had a cage with a tray that slid under it. She was even potty-trained. I sat on the bed that day with her, hugging her and remembering how I let The Mommy Part peek at Toby and me.

Of course, I was older before I realized God didn't make our bodies to share with seven people. They remained a secret for years, just like Daddy Chaz remained a bolted-down secret. But eventually it got crowded inside me, and my little girls started to act out. So, more secrets bloomed as a result. And these little girls began their venture to hurt, to get revenge, and take control, no matter who it affected.

Jasmine and I were young, but we knew what each other needed. We heard each other in an unspoken way. We decided to play in her room one afternoon. She didn't have as many dolls as I did, nor was her closet as big. But we found delight in each other. She'd lay on top of me and our thighs would be in-between each other's legs, and we'd rub and kiss, listening with our third ear for anyone. We wanted to make sure her mother was not coming, nor her drunken father. In all our ten-year-old ecstasy we never got caught.

After we had reached that place where it felt as if we fell off a cliff, only to soar to the sky, we'd talk. She'd let me into her world, and then I realized why I hated her father so. He had something similar, something I was familiar with—that same cold, hard gaze Daddy Chaz had. Jasmine's sheets weren't so white after all. The Mommy Part in me, the protector, wanted her father dead. I had to break off my love affair because the anger got so deep in me. I told Jasmine we were moving. I knew she'd see me around the neighborhood. But I couldn't tell her I didn't want to play anymore because I wanted to kill her father.

She was beautiful, Jasmine. She was a beautiful brown, like my mama. She had these tall slender legs, and a small frame. She looked as if she could be a model, unlike plain ol' Ginny. But I never saw any colored girls on the cover of those magazines that greeted Mama and me at the checkout counters. So Jasmine was always my personal centerfold.

I often wonder, when my children grow up, will they say my mama was once gay, loved a woman, even kissed her. Oh, but they must know it. They must know, it was only one woman. And pain, along with seven raging young girls inside of you, can make you crazy, see beauty in a diluted way.

I talked to The Mommy Part a lot. I talked to her about wanting to kill Jasmine's father, and about the separation of the two of us. It was so abrupt, just when it seemed we were really getting to understand each other's bodies, how we clicked. The Mommy Part said she did not care, that it was for our own good. I asked her, what did she know? She was only a little girl. She got very angry at me then, and went away into the corner of my mind that was her closet, her safe, warm place.

I decided to contact Emma again. I had a plan this time, a reason for our meeting. Since I could no longer drift away into the brownness of Jasmine's soft eyes, I decided to ter-rorize the tiny white girl across the street. But I needed help to do it. This is when I met The Mean Part. She was a sweet, but very vengeful little girl. I decided the right partner for the crime would be Emma. So, I started hanging out with her again.

The plan was to pretend we were Maggie's friends. That was her ugly name. After that was done and we gained Maggie's trust, we just beat her up. No warning, no name callin', just, "Hey Maggie!" And then, smack! She was a tiny thing; she kinda looked malnourished.

We weren't really beatin' her up, but more or less pushing our anger out on someone else. We had no warnings
regarding our misfortunes. Emma could not make her dad
stop lifting that bottle, and me, seemed I was doomed from
the start. So, why should she, this tiny, small Maggie, have
any warning. This was it, this was the thing. Let's do this!

I decided to make an all-girls' gang. Daddy Bubba had a
dirt bike gang called The Trojans. So, why not? By this time,
Emma and I met another Indian. Her name was Betty, but we
called her Blue Eagle. We became The Tuff Cookies, after Pat,
the rock singer. By this phase, my love for girls in a romantic
way diminished, and we became these "hot" girls. We chewed
gum, tried to wear tight jackets, pants, shirts; shoot, our
socks were even tight!

We stopped beating on Maggie, and went to trespassing,
climbing the neighbors' fruit trees and building a certified club
in an abandoned house up the street. This house was small, as
if it was for some slave that worked in the big house during the
day. It had a loft and small windows. The three of us swept and
dusted and picked up broken pieces of things all day. When it
was clean, it was also dark, so we had to leave. But early the
next day Emma and me were the first ones there. It was hard
to include Blue Eagle sometimes because her mom was such a
drunk that half the time Blue Eagle couldn't even get out of the
house. So, Emma and I had to move on without her.

Emma was the happiest there. I could tell. Her smile was different. It was not the same as when we went to any other adventure places, even Fantasy Island. Fantasy Island was a place that we entered through a row of bushes. Once we got in, there was a path. We followed this path for at least a mile. There were strawberries and fruit, and, of course, it was part of someone's garden, but these people were so rich, how could they miss a little fruit. Emma and I, whenever we made it through Fantasy Island without getting caught for trespassing, would smile—big.

When we listened to John Lennon's "Imagine," Emma would smile softly but tense, as if she really was trying to imagine all those lonely people, and why hadn't they come and gotten us. *We were lonely*. This song was us. She loved it. Not the Beatles, or anything they sang. It was just "Imagine" by John Lennon. But here in our little house, her smile was different because there was some peace mixed in with it. I don't ever remember seeing peace on Emma. But she had it in that small slave house.

This place became a safe haven for all of us, being that Emma's dad was an alcoholic and so was Blue Eagle's mom. It gave us a place to call our own, uninterrupted. Since I was the leader of the gang, they could not know about my imperfections, so I just blended in there. This became an art form for me, a habit, not to tell. Our gang was really a semi-circle of friends and a place where I felt I had control. All I really wanted was control, and to be a perfect Mama's girl. But inside me, those little girls were itching to get out and tell somebody of the crimes done to them, and more loudly, to me.

Nineteenth Street and our golden, rippled house became more of a tarred memory as I got older. But no matter how far I got away from it, it stayed close to me. It was as if I knew one day I'd be returning there, uncovering, picking up and putting together pieces, lots of broken pieces.

Mama met a man who worked with computers and seemed stable and she remarried. This, then, took us completely away and out of that house. We settled down in another house. It was further north, towards more blacks and whites. I had outgrown dolls and clubs, and tree climbing. But I still lusted for adventure, the plum fights, the cherry fights, and the excitement of running after we had crossed through and trampled someone's garden.

High school was around the corner and this meant more change. I was, by now, an expert at hiding my internal pain. I was so good, I fooled myself. Daddy Bubba went away to the Navy. I dated as any teenager would, only going to extremes to sleep around, making my life even more spotted and blemished. Sometimes these men were games to me. How many could I have? Sometimes it was a search for my father, and more than anything else, it was a manhunt to control and kill Daddy Chaz and all he had done to me. But I only hurt myself more.

I was an excellent student, despite all that. But by the time I was nineteen, I was pregnant, slowing my college plans down. What should have been done in two years, took three. Once I received that degree, I moved on to the university, and what should've taken two more years, took four. But at least I finished; I graduated!

The birth of my daughter, and moving out and away from Oregon, allowed for me to breathe. I didn't have to defend myself anymore, so I thought. I could also work on making things more perfect around me, like my grades and the way I kept my apartment. But as the schoolwork from the quarter piled on, no one could've warned me about the pressures I was going to face.

*Now, when ugly or evil tries to get in and control you, it still can't stand to be around love. So, immediately Sookie's connection to her mama had to go. Ugly still could not show its face around her. She cut herself off from the family, Sookie did. It was as if her mama never even birthed her. Once her mama came, singing Christmas carols, and Sookie, well I believe it was one of those evil little girls inside of her, called the police on her. The cops took her mama to jail for a couple of hours. Sookie had a restraining order put on her. Man, can you imagine? Sookie was so mixed up, so hurt. Secrets can be deadly. She then sunk into this world of her own. She was a single parent, full-time student with twenty credit hours, and the newness of being on her own. And those guys she messed around with just gave her a lot of crap, lots of it.*

As my daughter hit her terrific twos, I began to look at her as a little girl, and that was not good. It was not good because I began to see myself in her, instead of her. And I hated me because I was the dirty girl. I was full of flaws. I was the in-house family hooker, at someone else's free will, never my own. I remember sleeping around and waiting to experience the pain of losing my virginity, like the girls talked about in the locker room after dance class. But I never felt it, *never*. So, I looked at this small daughter of mine and saw all my imperfections.

One day we were coming home and she was, in my mind, walking too slow. I told her to hurry up, but she wouldn't go. So, I pushed her, and then I pushed her again, and again! Until she fell down. Those little girls inside me that I thought were asleep or dead for good awoke and rose up. The Mean Part laughed. The Mommy Part tried to hold her back because she saw this wasn't no man attacking us. It was a small child, yet The Mean Part is blind and just wanted to beat and kick this little girl. The Mommy part didn't let her, but took over and picked up the little girl, my daughter, and told her she was sorry, so sorry.

At two years old, my daughter did not know what was going on, at least not right away. But The Mommy Part knew I needed help. This was way beyond Jasmine, Emma, climbing trees, and listening to breathing walls. This was dangerous, a danger zone. So she decided to get me help. And when all the other little girls inside me turned their heads for a moment, she jumped out and did just that.

*This story gets hard to tell at times. My heart opens up and she either wants to run, spit, or quit. But she steadies herself and she continues. She floats on, moves forward as Mama told her she must do that day in the kitchen. 'Cause see, there's beauty in this. God shows His face, He really does, and she wants you to hang in there for that part, 'cause it comes, it really does come. And it's darkest before the dawn, right? I know it's been dark a long time, but joy really does come in the morning. But before joy you must clean your soul up, sweep, mop, and let it dry out. Then you have to put on that shine. Yet, sometimes before you even get to the shine, you have to do some strippin' of the floor, pull up the tile. So, stay with her, y'all, and you'll see how this thing turns out, how ugly is forced to die.*

Those outbursts frightened me. Something awful was brewing in me. What kind of anger was this? This was my daughter, my blood. I once heard a lady say, "I stopped looking for my family to be family and just looked for them to be human. People say blood is thicker than water, but blood is just blood and nothing more." But to me, this was my daughter, my blood. I helped create her, and I did not want to hurt her, ever. I made some calls at work one morning. I was working as a journalist part-time. I acted as if I was someone else. I called those anonymous-type groups and pretended I had a friend who needed help. When I realized they really could not tell me much but needed to talk to the victim, I finally told them it was me. Parents Anonymous was a beginning point, but the real work began in therapy, where I learned that those little girls I thought I rescued, were just *parts of me all chopped up.*

I asked my therapist, "What does this chopped up stuff mean?"

She said, "It's a survival method you developed to deal with your pain."

*My* pain! Why, does it always have to be my pain, mine all by myself? I wonder why I didn't tell my mama? Would Daddy Chaz really have killed his own mother? I did not know how to handle this, these seven different little girls inside of me. To me they were real people. I was sure I'd never get well. I was sure that I'd see this therapist lady forever, but she got me to talking, to remembering. So with my eyes open, I took a deep breath and took her in, into that house.

It was night. Mama had left for Geneva's. I was upstairs in my room. I had built a tent out of her sheets, and went downstairs to get three of her dining room chairs. I used phonebooks to bolt the sheets down onto the pads of the chairs. Then, I crawled under it.

This time would be different, though. Instead of dolls, I'd go get her small TV out of her room, hook it up in mine and watch it, under my heaven. He came in. He got under the tent with me. There was a gum commercial on at the time for Big Red chewing gum.

He said to me, "Mona, come here."

It was always Mona, too; he never called me Sookie, maybe 'cause that's what Daddy named me, and he needed to separate himself from that. Anyway, I was already there, so what? I thought he just wanted to watch TV, but no.

He told me, "Let's try to kiss like the people did in the commercial. But so nobody will see us, we should go into your closet."

My closet, my Narnia?

I got up, why not?

He shut the closet door and told me, "Now take your pants off!"

It was dark and I did not like the dark.

He told me, "Remember what I said last time."

Elaine, that was my therapist's name, asked me, "So this was not the first time?"

I did not answer her. I just went on because I could not stop.

I pulled my pants down.

He told me, "Touch it," but I didn't want to.

I said, "It's too prickly, too pokey."

"Do it!" he commanded.

So I did, but quickly.

Then he told me, "Lay down, *lay down!*"

I did, instantly. I couldn't breathe; all the air around me was leaving, going into the walls.

"Stop! Wait for me," I yelled to the walls, "Please stop!"

He mounted me, like some kid on a horse.

"It hurts, please . . ." but the rest of my sentence never came out because he covered my mouth like some criminal.

He thrust his pokey thing into me and my insides felt like they exploded. It was dry. It was hot. There was no air because it done left and went into those walls, where I wanted to be. He left eventually. I stayed, legs open, staring at the ceiling. How was I going to get across the hall? There was blood.

I don't know. It may have been the little people I rescued that carried me to the bathroom to wash. It may have been an angel, but I made it. Then the world was black, even my pink bedroom Mama worked so hard to paint.

Elaine was there, just looking at me. She did not push me, she never pushed me to tell. I wanted to cry. She knew there was more, but not on that day, just not on that day.

My daughter is a love child. Her father was an older man from Jamaica, part of my quest to find my father, in an altered sort of way. She was two when all the throwing up of memories and flashbacks started. She, again, reminded me so much of myself, parts of me just wanted her gone. The Mean Part, so self-consumed, tried many times to make this child not exist. She failed, thank God.

I never knew seven people inside you could be so different. It was like they all had their own minds. Like Mama said, it's not good to entertain spirits. But this was not the case. My mind split up into pieces, in order to survive and try to make sense out of the hot, the dry, and the blackness, so much blackness. I had to learn how to tell the difference between the multiple personalities, learn the signs of each one of them and what would be the trigger to make them come out and try to rule the world.

The Mean Part, she tried to drown my daughter once. Yup, right there in the bathroom of family housing at the university. I was just kneeling over the side of the tub washing her small body, her hair and then suddenly, The Mean Part came out of nowhere and tried to make my daughter suck in all that warm water. I don't know what broke the hold I had on her. I don't know why I stopped, but I remember who and what I saw. I saw me, little me, and I wanted me dead. So very dead. Oh, how it hurts to tell some of this, to think that at this moment in some person's mind I could be considered a criminal. But there is a difference: I got help.

They call my daughter Shuga. So good, for her soul is very sweet. She was, of course, my mama's child in a special way. When because of all the fear, I screamed, "Abortion!" Mama screamed right back at me, "You can make it."

Mama was shocked at first when I got pregnant at nineteen. She went over all the milestones of how she taught me to be careful. She asked me what happened, but I never really had an answer for her. I even tried to lie when she first asked if I was pregnant. Soon enough, the mere thought of abortion flew by me, and I shot it. I made it explode into a million pieces, sending it right back to hell, letter by individual letter, until the entire word slithered away for good.

Pregnant at nineteen was an awakening for me. Not only did the little girls in my mind awake after the birth, but a part of me was trying to become a woman, someone stable, someone that somebody could eventually love. Yet, it seemed as though I just kept making bigger messes. My daughter's father has never seen her. He has never even heard her voice, and yet she was a result of my quest to find my daddy in a funny sort of way. No one found their dads. No one.

*I have to keep steppin' in. It's okay, though, 'cause it's our story and I'm part of Sookie and this is the raw truth, all of it. You would've thought gettin' pregnant and all would've brought Sookie so much closer to her mama, 'specially with such a complicated birth. Sookie kept hollerin' this stuff about going to see her great-grandma in heaven right there on the delivery room table. Her mama was fightin' the whole time, prayin', tellin' her she had to stay, that she could not leave her to raise the baby alone. But Sookie was determined to die the day her daughter was born. In some ways, she did die.*

*But after some years, Sookie was coming alive again. She began to fight ugly, and I saw myself that ugly was not going to have a fat chance in hell, trying to get Sookie down any-more. She kept going to therapy. Day after day, week after week. She would even get pulled over sometimes for speed-ing. She'd try to hold those little girls in until she got into Elaine's office. But sometimes they'd spill out and push the gas petal real hard.*

Sorry, officer. Man! I could not seem to get to Elaine's fast enough. The Mean Part broke loose and tried to kill me. But it was my daughter who saved me, my daughter! Imagine that. I was just there in my white-walled apartment. I had a nightmare *again*. I wanted out! I was sure I couldn't do this anymore. This healing stuff was for the birds. I had already pushed my sweet mama away. I had no strength, not even the strength of a powerful, black woman, who came from a strong line of history. I did not have that umbilical connection, or so I thought.

It went this way. I went to the kitchen and grabbed the knives. It was Daddy Chaz I wanted to kill, not me. But since he had been inside of me, robbed me, I figured I could kill the part of him that manifested and swam around in me. I was sure to do this. I was sure this was it; I would be free. But my daughter, at two, had climbed out of her crib and come to me. I told her to stand back. But she did not. Instead, she looked me directly in the eyes and said clearly, very clearly, "Mommy, please don't do that, I need you."

My eyes opened wide. How did she know? How could she just suddenly speak so clearly, so directly? But she did. Then she came into my personal zone. She broke through my walls with no warning and put her small arms around me. I grabbed her back and cried over her shoulder. She held me like Mama would've done. I guess it was Mama. Someone, somewhere had to be prayin' for me 'cause the end never came for me. But a lot of facing did. I had to face a lot of facts and truths about who I was, where I came from and that I was not a prisoner. I had to go into that house over and over again. The nightmares were the best way to get in.

*Sookie could dream. Boy, some of those dreams would bring tears right to her eyes. Some of them would make her hit, kick, and punch in her sleep. Some of them seemed so real, she'd wake up in the morning, just lookin' over her shoulder. I guess she was lookin' for him, you know, Daddy Chaz. He was never there, but you couldn't have told her that at the time. What with those little girls stompin' all over the place, Sookie could not hear. She just wanted them to stop, but then she got to drawin' these pictures, too. She said they were what she saw at night, and man, I never knew someone who was supposed to be your brother could look so scary. I felt sorry for Sookie. But she doesn't want anybody feelin' sorry for her. Yet she does want people to know, to get stronger and to know that there is sunshine after the rain. Sookie, like I said, began to get stronger. Ugly sure better watch out now.*

The dreams.

There were many. Some short, some long. Some dry, some hot.

# Three

---

The dreams. It used to be that I had journals and journals of those dreams, those nightmares, those flashbacks. I would leave them around the house with those breathing walls and hope that Mama would pick one up. Then maybe she'd know, find out, and somehow help me to escape. You know it's God's wrath we are supposed to suffer. But mine was Daddy Chaz's. Sure, I grew up, had a child, and went on to get my second degree. Daddy Chaz probably went on to making somebody else's life miserable. For all I know, he may have gotten help, but his wrath followed me.

They say every time you sleep with someone, you pick up part of their spirit. So, I figured whatever jumped into Daddy Chaz at that house, whatever was living in him to make him act so ugly, was living in me, too. It was a *big* ugly, too, strong enough to drip into my sleep.

These dreams became keys to putting together the whole picture. They became helpmates, to get me to be strong enough, so I could do something healthy with those little girls inside me. At first, I had to learn they could not control me.

There was one dream in particular. I was in the breathing house. I was walking through each room. The rooms were empty, all except mine. When I got to the closet, I saw the blood stain on the floor. I backed up to run down the stairs and it was as if I felt him behind me. I went to the front door, the door Mama always told us not to go out of. I opened it and ran. I ran, and ran, and ran.

When I opened my eyes I was in my apartment looking at the walls. The only difference was they were not breathing, I was. I almost called one of the parents who went to Parents Anonymous. They were good to call at any hour because most of them went through things, too. They were alcoholics, abusive, hurt, and chopped up, like I was. But I didn't. I waited to speak to Elaine. When I got to her, she had me go back into the house. She had me look into each room again, and when I got to the blood, she had me see that it was a stain. She had me turn and get bigger, so big that I busted through the roof of that house. She had me step on Daddy Chaz, so he couldn't chase me or scare me. She put me in control. She said I had to learn to make myself bigger, each and every time he came after me in my sleep.

A lot of times I wanted my mama. I wanted to call her on those nights and tell her, but something was always in the way. I just figured it was nothing but ugly and The Mean Part standing in the way. But I also was not in the place to fully believe Daddy Chaz would not still go after Mama and kill her. I wanted so badly to be sure, though.

I wrote a story when I was ten. I kept this story, along with the other ones, in a homemade book. I drew all the pictures to go with each story, too. I used color and detail, because maybe through the detail somebody would know the secrets I held and help me out.

In this story, I was a little girl whose mother and father never listened to her. It was this girl's wish that she could fly away. She would go to bed night after night and wish she could fly. So one evening as she knelt down asking God for this favor, she also made it clear what she wanted to be. She wanted to be a butterfly. This way, when she changed she would be a new creature—beautiful, vibrant, and full of color. She would no longer be the dirty girl. Well, when her parents came in to check on her the next morning, because it had been so quiet, all they found was a butterfly in the place where their daughter slept. There happened to be a crack in the window, and in the wink of an eye, the little girl flew. She flew out the window and was never seen again, except maybe in the meadows of the places where there is heaven on earth.

Oh, I wrote lots of stories like these. My favorite thing was to fly. I wanted to fly so badly. Birds seemed to have it easy. And it even says in the Bible how God always provides for the birds. I believe He called them sparrows. Writing stories became my thing. But Mama never picked them up. She never even picked up the journals I laid around. Come to find out years on top of years later, she did not want to invade my privacy. Imagine that! Seems kind of ironic. After Daddy Chaz rummaged through my privacy, she didn't want to invade it. She may have been able to salvage it.

But the dreams never really let up. They just got scattered around, where chunks would come at me at one time. I began to think I was obsessed with this whole thing about Daddy Chaz. It seemed this was taking so much of my time, my awake and my sleep time. I would awaken, fists flying, screaming, "*No!*" Sometimes I screamed in my apartment, in the dark, into my pillow. But I wasn't obsessed. I had to go through the unrest to heal. I had to go deep in order to heal. I had to find out the true reasons for all my unrest in the night and the day. So, still in my twenties, I was screaming.

Flashbacks began each time I tried to settle with a man. There the two of us would be, getting serious, sometimes I thought I was close to marriage, but no, not me. It would usually be about three in the morning when my arms would start swinging. Then I'd scream, aloud this time. Sure, whoever my boyfriend was at the time would hold my arms and me until I came back. Usually, by then one of the little girls had jumped out.

The Parents Anonymous number was always close, but those folks began to seem more and more distant from my hell. Yet Elaine knew these little girls, and she'd talk to them, no matter the hour.

She'd say, "Hello?"

Then she'd go in for the kill, but she always made sure my daughter was safe first.

She'd ask, "Who am I speaking to?"

It would be The Mommy Part, because she was smart, see, and she loved my daughter and me.

The Mommy Part would go on to tell her how The Mean Part was beatin' Daddy Chaz, but she was really hurtin' me, Sookie.

Then Elaine would ask, "What happened? Why does The Mean Part feel she needs to protect Sookie?"

The Mommy Part was always honest. She'd tell her, "'Cause he came at her again."

*Darn nightmares.*

*You know she wanted to say something else. But "darn nightmares" was right. Hard as Sookie tried to tell Elaine* some of them nightmares, the further they seemed to run. I guess ugly figured she was gettin' smart and using them nightmares to get well. Sookie didn't want to keep livin' in the past. She wanted to move on. She wanted to be loved, get married. She wanted her mama. But things seemed so bent out of shape. She felt like she hid too long. She just kept pushing her mama back. That took a lot, too.

See, her mama didn't just give up so easily. She came after her only daughter, she tried to fight, to get her back, to see why she hated her so suddenly and abruptly. Nothing worked, so Sookie thought. But while ugly was trying to consume her, her mama met a lady named Benita. And the two of them put things together, then they started prayin' for Sookie. They got on their knees and started prayin', 'cause they knew something was wrong . . . just what, was the question.

Sookie's mama had Lupus and would get sick off and on. She was stressed out; who wouldn't be? That was her only daughter, and Sookie, you could tell she was dying inside. Her mama didn't want to bury her, she didn't want to outlive any of her four children. So, she did the only fightin' she knew how. She started to pray. And this praying bruised her knees. This prayin' put her to sleep at night. She believed. She believed no matter how long it was going to take that God would bring her daughter back. The beautiful thing, though, is that her friend would pray with her. 'Cause, there is power in numbers, 'specially when you're fightin' an ugly as big as the one that entered Sookie and her Daddy Chaz.

Things got a little altered in my times with Elaine. Those dreams began to get real confusing. They put *all* my daddy brothers to blame. They put them in scenes, where they were molesting me. They put my sweet mama in some, where she was beating up on me or hollering at me. But the truth be told, none of them ever hurt me. Ugly was just that, and it was getting discovered, so it tried to scatter the true story all over the place and put lies on others that had nothing but love for me. This ugly hoped I would stay away from my family forever, with these lies behind it. Daddy Bubba and Daddy Tee never put a hand on me. Mama never did anything out of the ordinary. Shoot, Mama wouldn't even let Daddy spank me. She said it wasn't right. Men shouldn't be hitting on their baby girls. But there was a time when Mama came down on me, but that's because she didn't know. Mama just didn't know.

There was a man named Dirk. He took a little eye to my mama after Daddy left and Daddy Chaz began his creepin'. The doorbell rang, and I had been planning this all day, so I ran to get it. Dirk was tall and thin. His eyes kinda sagged.

He said, "Hi," then immediately, "Is your mom home?"

But it was not gonna be that easy for him. I asked him, "What do you want with my mama?"

He said, "I want to take her out."

But I told him, "No you don't!" right to his face. I said, "You don't want to do nothing but rape my mama, you b____."

By that time Mama was making her way down the steps, probably leaning against those breathing walls. She called, "Sookie! Go up to your room!"

Stupid man! If it wasn't for him, Mama would've stayed home that night! I know she would've. She spanked me soon after that. She told me I had to stay in my room the rest of the night. This is when I met Moan. Out of all the little girls inside of me, she wept the most. She didn't cry; she just wept. I have no idea what she thought those tears were gonna do, they sure didn't save us that night Mama went out. I tried writing, too. But I just ended up scribbling. And Moan, she was out most of the time, making puddles everywhere, with them stupid tears.

*Dreaming sucked for Sookie. She got to a point where she didn't want to close her eyes. She got to a point where she didn't even want the men that came knocking, risking the very chance that Sookie would probably be beatin' on them by three in the morning. She tried to tell the men she* almost got serious with what happened to her. But it seems as though they just took it lightly, almost as if she was just crazy. So she stopped trying to tell them. She eventually learned how to get bigger and always crush Daddy Chaz in those dreams. She also learned ways to go back into the house and rescue the little girls, put them in safe places in her mind.

The one to tame, though, was The Mean Part. She had to lock that little girl behind glass walls in her mind. The walls had to be glass so you could see through them, so The Mean Part would not think you forgot about her. But it had to stay locked a lot of the time. The other little girls inside her, The Twins, Blue, The Mommy Part, Moan and Mona were all okay just as long as they stayed in their little warm pockets inside Sookie's mind. The Twins, though, had a fetish. They always wanted to kill Sookie. Sookie drew a picture of them once. They were cute little girls, with orange bows in their hair, but one always wore a noose around her neck. She was the Suicide Part.

Blue, well, she was a funny one. She stayed in a box a lot, where she knew nobody but her could fit. The Mommy Part roamed around a lot. She was just looking out for everyone, including Sookie. And Moan was waiting. She never did much to try to hurt Sookie, never even showed out that much. But she, like all the others, was there.

Sookie began these complex exercises with Elaine, though. They were eventually to help Sookie know she was just one person. Yup! Just one! Me, I believe it was the praying her mama was doing that really broke through.

# *Four*

I don't know exactly when things started to change for me. But I got hungry. I got hungry for something more. So I got into what I thought was a church. I figured, if anything, this would help me. But do you know ugly can disguise itself? I still had not called Mama yet. I was still running. And in the process I ran right into this cult, but you couldn't have told me it was a cult at first. I was singing and praying right along with these people. I just knew Daddy Chaz was gone and all the little girls, too. My sessions with Elaine had almost stopped. She thought I was doing better. But the lines were always open. I was the one who backed off for a while.

I started taking my daughter to these services. Man, they had this lady there, and they claimed she was telling you words that were directly from God Himself, but the only reason I know they were lies is that everything she professed crumbled. It crumbled and took my journals, and drawings right along with them, making my story about Daddy Chaz seem all that much harder to tell. They told me first to get rid of everything.

You must know there was this sweet black lady who sat with me on the lawn of a daily newspaper that told me about God. And then she looked me in the eyes and told me that one day I would have to tell about this cult. She said it was important that others know things like that exist. I shuddered inside. Who would I tell and would they really care that I almost, once again, was lost in the wind of my traumas.

*Oh, but they must know, because all this is related, see. It all twines together and makes sense, and then God steps in with all His power and MIGHT, and you'll see. Just stay with me during all the tellin'. I never knew there would be so much tellin'.*

I thought it would be a cold day in hell before I got mixed up in some mess like this! These people swore they heard straight from God Himself. Man, the minister and his wife would have that little building packed, just calling people up and telling them what they said they heard the Lord saying about them, and these people would believe them. It was like free fortune telling. Man, a lot of these people were young. They were young and looking for something; that's why I fit right in. I thought all of it was for real, too.

The husband would preach and the wife, well, she was the different one. She claimed to have this gift of prophecy. And boy, did folks live off every word that fell from those dark lips of hers. She, at first, reminded me of a witch, but I kinda just pushed that thought into the back of my mind. See, I didn't want her to know what I was thinking and have her try to condemn me or something. At the time, it seemed like she had that much power.

She would call people out from the audience, saying, "Hey! Yeah, you." And they would stand up. Then she'd go on to say what God was telling her to tell them. She'd say things like they need to give up what they had, and how we need to take care of her because she is one of God's chosen. She'd tell us how we needed to support her because it was our duty.

She told this one couple that God was gonna bless them, that she saw them in a Jag, furs, and many things like these. Man, that couple must've given everything they had, money and whatever else they could get their hands on.

One time she had the whole building full of folks down on their knees. Me, I kept peeking up, trying to see where she was because I was kinda scared of this woman. But because she seemed to know everything about everyone's past and future, I'd close my eyes back tight again. But as everyone knelt down, she went on hollering, yelling, and saying things like, "I told you!" She was accusing us of not being a faithful people and telling us that God was real angry with us. Boy, people followed this woman, too, 'cause they believed her every word, being that the Lord was speaking directly to her, so she said.

Well, if I had any sense at all, I lost it on account of this woman and her fortune telling, because that's what it came down to be. And these people used the Bible, too! They used it like a tool, but it was actually a really bad weapon because they took everything out of context. They would find little scriptures, and quotes, and sayings, and throw them in with all their fortune telling about folks' lives and what they were to do with them.

When it came to me, they were telling me that my husband was in this building (the church). So who wouldn't look around? I did and I ended up spottin' this fat, bumpy-skinned guy. They called him Harvey. So we went out. But we didn't really go out. We just went back and forth to that church and he would talk to me and tell me God was leading him, and that he was going to be really rich. He said God was going to send him a big check in the mail.

During the course of this church-going, he did ask me to marry him. Well, I said yes. I didn't know him at all. But this lady guaranteed us that she was hearing directly from God. So I figured if God said it, I must have to do it. But that was not enough.

He was in front of my apartment and started reading something from the Bible. After he was done, he asked me, "Do you know what all that meant?"

I told him, "No."

He told me, "It means that you have to get rid of everything you own. Everything! Your things are possessed by the devil."

Now, today I know this is crazy, but back then I couldn't hear.

Why, I had those little girls inside me hiding out. I missed my mama. I was secretly trying to kill Daddy Chaz and forever looking for my daddy in men. Man, it was too much! Now, the devil was in my stuff! So I was shaking, but everything, things I had since I was a little girl, ended up in the dumpster. All my journals, the ones I used to lay around for Mama to find, along with all my drawings, poems, pictures, clothes, and shoes, were now gone. The only things I kept were my daughter's things.

Then the clincher was that I was not to go back to my apartment, nor was I to drive my car, because, according to them and that witch lady, the devil was in them all. So I returned the car to the guy I was buying it from, no words or anything. I just took the car to the house, left the keys in it and drove off with this man, who they said was to be my husband—because God said so.

The rent went unpaid at my apartment. Harvey said God told him that I was to give all my money to him. Now, I was thinking the whole time, "God is saying to do this." So I thought I'd better not do anything different or something bad might happen to me, the dirty girl. I was told to quit my job. So there I was, with my daughter's things in this guy Harvey's house. And the house was cold as winter itself. My things were gone and all these people kept doing were making promises to him and me. So I was waiting.

After they conducted the marriage, I didn't want to sleep with him, but I had to. Yet, after that one night, I tried everything in my power not to sleep with him again. This guy got stranger and stranger. He began to spend a lot of time away; and if he wasn't away, he was at the cold house on the phone. He would tell the mortgage people that soon, soon he'd have this check from his father. And he meant his Father, God in heaven.

One day he left and I started to look around. Maybe it was The Mommy Part coming out, because she knew something wasn't right. So, I looked down at his mail. I saw unemployment stubs, unpaid bills; everything was up for closure, even his house! The Mommy Part jumped out and started looking for a way to get my daughter and me out of that house. I realize now, all I had to do was leave, contact one of my old boyfriends, like the one I left before I got into all of this mess. But I didn't leave. Oh no, ugly wouldn't have had it be so easy.

Harvey came back. When I asked him if he had a job, he said, "No, but everything is going to be alright."

He was taking all of my money and God was soon going to give him this big check. Shoot, he even drove me out north to this small suburban community and had a lady show us a brand new house. I was eating this up, until he started asking me questions.

We would be driving in the car, and if I said something, he would ask me, "Did God tell you to say that?"

I, of course, said, "I don't know, I was just talking to you."

Then he told me, "If God didn't tell you to say it, you shouldn't speak at all."

On one of those nights I was trying to act asleep, so I wouldn't have to sleep with him, I had my head under the covers, trying to breath some heat around me. I heard him on the phone with the pastor of that church. He was telling him that he didn't think I was the one. What one? Anyway, he told the "pastor" that I would not sleep with him; he told him that he thought I was an impostor! What was this? I got scared then.

But who could I go to, to get out? I was so deep in mess again. Well, what I managed to do one evening, since these people claimed to be so close to God, saying He gave them direct orders regarding everybody and every move, I decided to pray. I closed the bedroom door. My daughter was asleep. He knocked, but I told him he could not come in. While he was getting angrier, I asked God, the God Mama taught me about, to help me.

I got on my knees against that big bed on that cold wooden floor. The first thing I did was cry. I cried silently, because this guy was turning into some kind of madman. I had locked the bedroom door, because there were times I'd be in the room and I'd catch him peeking through the cracks of the door at me. His only comeback for this behavior was that he was watching me because he believed I was not his wife. He said he thought I was an impostor, the devil. That's all I needed; now I'm the devil? Being a dirty girl was not enough!

Anyway, I locked that door. As I cried, I asked God over and over again to help me. The madman was outside the door yelling. I believe something was watching over my daughter because she never woke up. Maybe it was all that real praying Mama was doing, the prayers that bruised her knees so. Anyway, this Harvey guy called his mother over. Then he called that witch lady and her husband who was the "pastor."

They didn't come, but his mother did. She kept talking to me through the door. She was telling me to come out, to come out, please! But I didn't. I was locked in that room asking God to help me. Because the way Mama taught us, this man they said was God, the man telling them do all these things, takes everyone's things, takes everyone's money, I just knew it couldn't have been my God. Because anything of God could not feel so alien. No matter how bad we may feel inside, no matter how mixed up, God doesn't feel bad, and I felt bad inside.

It was over an hour. My eyes were red. I did not get up, though, until his mother had left and it was quiet. He was sitting on that black couch by then. He was out there crying, too. He said he was praying for God to save him from me. Imagine that! He told me to stay away from him, that I had to go.

He stayed out in the freezing living room that night. He then got up very early the next day and left the house. I took his car and my daughter and I drove away to what I thought was nowhere. But I realized my daughter was sick so I took her to Children's Hospital and, believe it or not, they admitted us! I had a place to stay and felt safe, for a minute. But ugly was going fast by then, it was gettin' nervous. The Mommy Part, since she could breathe now, since she was warm, she picked up that phone and called my mama. She called her! After all this time, she called Mama and put me on the phone.

*Now grace and mercy steps in. It gets even bigger later, but Sookie, she ain't seen her mama in a long while and now there is this crazy stuff going on, not to mention her weak mind and all those little girls inside it.*

*Would her mama listen? You bet she listened. Ugly must've wanted to bust straight through into the hospital Sookie and her daughter were at, but hah! Nothing is stronger than a praying mama, 'specially when two are together, and you must remember she had that sweet friend praying right along with her the whole time, all those years and months and days.*

*Now, with Sookie havin' pushed her mama away so after Sookie shut down on her mama, trust was an issue—only a little one, though.*

*Sookie's mama came right out and asked her, "Are you gonna run away anymore? I can't handle it anymore. You have to choose. Either you're gonna be part of the family or you aren't gonna be part of the family."*

*Her mama told her right away that she can't take no more pain 'cause Lupus is a sneaky thing, and that's what her mama had. It functions off of stress; it loves stress. And Sookie's mama, well, she was really stressed about her baby girl and why it seemed like she didn't love her anymore.*

*Sookie dug down real deep in her heart, The Mommy Part and all the little girls were watching, and she said, "I promise there won't be no more running."*

'Man, her mama must've had the strength of eagle's wings, 'cause she said, "Okay, we have some fightin' to do."

Now, she wasn't talking about no fistfight. No, no. She was talking about some real spiritual fightin'. So, Sookie closed her eyes and hung on tight because she had no idea what deliverance felt like, none whatsoever.

Well, this Harvey guy showed his bumpy face again. Yup, came straight to the hospital demanding that Sookie give him the keys to the car. She put up a small fuss, though, see, 'cause he was leaving her with nothing again. She tried to tell him that she needed to get her daughter's clothes, but he didn't care. He told her straight to her face, she would need a court order before she got into that house again, along with police escorts. 'Cause in his mind, she was an impostor, full of the devil himself.

Yeah, I know I must've been crazy. But when folks go to talking about God and all, and swearing they're hearing straight from Him, what are you to do? It seemed like my ears were plugged a mighty long time. But when I was away from it all, in the quietness of the hospital room, I realized that I was just trying to find a solution to all my muck, a cure for the dirty girl. Little did I know the real cure, the real deliverance had nothing to do with track shoes, and kicking up dust along with kicking the people who loved you. I had to learn to love myself, but how?

It seems as though, after Daddy Chaz did his creeping, all my intentions of ever loving anybody left, except for loving my mama. I always loved her. In all my nightmares, in all my days and years away, she was there in my heart. But I wanted to make sure she was safe forever, 'cause Daddy Chaz threatened to kill her and my dad, if I ever told. I did not want to see her dead, nor my daddy, for that matter. Even though it had been more years on top of years since I'd seen my daddy. As long as I knew he and my mama were alive somewhere in the world, I was okay with that, completely okay, with keeping my mouth shut.

My daughter stayed in the hospital a total of seven days. They needed to put a tube into her stomach for her to be fed through. They said all the fluids were going into her lungs and this would be the only way to feed her for a while. They said most of the times these things correct themselves, but they would keep watch on her. I now knew what the reason was for her not breathin' too clearly all those nights in that cold house. While I stayed and waited, and learned about this feeding tube, I also looked for a job. Yes, a job. I also tore the papers up trying to find a place to stay.

That madman had taken all my money, even my income tax return. That was actually when he really started acting funny, saying I had to go. Mama went on to tell me that this whole church thing he was a part of was a scam. She told me they were probably doing that type of thing to more people than just me. She said with people like that, they brainwash you, get you to believe God is speaking to them, so they can control you and reap lots of material benefits. I guess it was a clever scam.

I noticed no real old people in that church, ever. It was always just a bunch of young folks, looking for a way to make their dreams come true. When Mama flew up to help me out of the mess and help me to get a divorce going, I knew God had heard my prayers in that cold house, on that wooden floor of Harvey's room. That got my attention. But after all this confusion, and people saying they were hearing from God, I was scared.

I didn't want to go back to church, ever, not ever! But since I knew the real God heard my cry for help, I never stopped talking to Him at night. I may not have been in some building each Sunday singing praises, but I never stopped praying—not until later.

My dreams have a way with me, and I started dreaming about those cult people. Especially that witch lady who told everybody's past and present. She was always wearing black in my sleep, always after me, telling me not to tell anybody about her or I would die. This happened for a long time after I had gotten the divorce and was in my own place.

I was working at a local newspaper. It seemed like my life was getting back on track. Yet this witch lady kept on coming to me in my dreams. Sometimes I'd awaken real hot from running in my sleep. Sometimes I swung, like I did at Daddy Chaz in my dreams. I was getting tired. The little girls inside me were starting to fidget.

The Mean Part somehow got from behind those glass walls and busted through, right out of me. She was gonna strangle that witch lady. But it didn't quite happen like that. The Mean Part, well, she figured she got a hold on me, since I was tired, tired of dreaming, tired of all the threats and so forth.

So, one night after a nightmare, I lay awake. The witch lady seemed as if she was right outside the big living room window of my third-floor apartment. She had on that nasty, black dress again. She just floated outside there, with her big brown eyes and dark lips. She kept telling me to jump, that I would then be free. She kept telling me God wants me to jump, that He's ready for me. So I was getting frustrated again. It was three in the morning and I had told myself that it was time for me to go. I was gearing myself up to jump!

See, earlier that day, while sitting in my car, I had already told the devil he could have me, forget it, just have me. Little did I know how dangerous that was. Ugly must've been excited at this point. It must've been ecstatic. Well, the phone rang. Out of nowhere, it just rang. I picked the phone up and the witch lady, well, she disappeared, but my thoughts didn't.

I finally realized why she disappeared so fast. It was Mama that called, and we know by now how much effect she has on ugly, any kind of ugly. She asked me, "How are you doing?"

But I just couldn't say much more than, "Why are you calling me so late?"

She just kept asking me, "How are you doing?"

I told her, "I'm fine."

But she heard more in my voice and asked again, so I told her I was going to do it. I told her that I had condemned myself earlier and that I was going to go now.

Boy, Mama jumped in and told me that I was not going anywhere. She told me, "Tell me what you said in the car about challenging the devil to take you."

I told her, "I told the devil I'd surrendered and that he could have me."

She was taken by this, and told me, "You ask for forgiveness right away."

I told her, "I can't."

Man, these people, these so-called "church" people, had taken my everything. They took my home, my old Winnie-the-Pooh lunch box, my security blanket, my pride, my dignity, and the little self-esteem I had left. They almost took my daughter's health in that cold house, too!

My heart was aching. It ached so bad. Mama raised her voice slightly and told me again to pray. She said no matter how bad it may seem, even if I never go back into another church in my life, that I cannot give up on praying. She said after Daddy left, she may not have had much, but she had her prayers, and they put food on the table and clothes on our backs.

I knew those "church" people were fakes. I knew it was all part of a little scheme that was part of a big scheme that was part of a bigger scheme. Mama said to have faith and the Holy Spirit would look after me. I was crying again. Seems as though Moan came out, and started her weeping. Man, I wish she would just get in the box with Blue. Mama listened to me, the way she used to in the kitchen of that house with those breathing walls. It felt good to be home.

# Five

Now, Sookie was in for a real treat. 'Cause her mama was back, see, and this whole thing was gonna straighten out. It was not gonna be crooked anymore. Sookie was in for an awakening. Those little girls, too! 'Cause things were about to get told. Ugly was about to get its behind beat. There isn't anything worse than getting beat with a switch off one of those bushes in the yard. And Sookie's mama, well, she had a switch—a direct-line-into-God switch.

She started spending more time on the phone with Sookie. She came up to see her more, now that the doors were open, and she kept tellin' Sookie to pray. She was sure God would hear her. But the key here is that Sookie had to be ready for God's answers, 'cause her mama assured her she would not like some of them. So, Sookie struck out to pray on *her knees in the evenings, and if she fell asleep, she'd catch up with Jesus in the morning. And her world began to change more. Her world began to open up 'cause it had to swallow this ugly up. No chewing necessary, it had to be swallowed up, and this had to start with Sookie tellin' her mama 'bout Daddy Chaz and those little girls she rescued.*

Oh, Mama didn't know. She just didn't know. It was a lukewarm day when Mama came to see me in that small apartment of mine. She had sat awhile, talked awhile, even ate some smoked salmon I had cooked. My daughter was out playing, leaving just the two of us. Just us and the sunshine breaking through the wooden fence of the back way where the pool was. Mama would glance at me every now and then. I had cut my hair real short and she was trying to get used to it. She said she was very shocked, seeing that she'd nursed my hair each day of my childhood until it gracefully brushed my shoulders.

"Mama, I have something to tell you."

She looked over at me, with that light tan, flawless skin of hers. Her eyes kinda sparkled some, and I took strength in them. I went into the room and got out a picture I had drawn recently.

She asked me, "Who's that?"

I told her, "Just look at it."

She told me, "Well the eyes, they are so big, almost demonic, and definitely scary."

I told her, "It's someone you know. Please look at it and think."

So she did, and in a wink of an eye she said softly under her breath, "Oh, my God!"

That was it. I looked at her and asked her, "Do you know who it is now?"

She said, "If I'm looking right, that's Chaz. Why does he look like that?"

I looked at the ground. I wanted to quit, to call Elaine, but The Mommy Part jumped out. "He raped us! I mean he raped me."

Mama immediately said, "What?"

So The Mommy Part said it again, "He raped me."

Mama stood up and asked me, "Why didn't you ever tell me? Why? I never thought something like this could ever happen. I was so careful."

I was wondering, ". . . she was careful . . ." What did this have to do with her being careful?

Then she said, "You always seemed so happy all the time. You were so creative."

I was so creative. Man, she had the key right there on the brink of her lips and still never caught any of my hints, my silent cries for help, all the journals I left around. They may have taken you to another place, a world of make believe, but they held secret codes to my chambers.

I went on to ask her, "Do you remember the time after you remarried, when you stood in the kitchen of your new house and told me Chaz was coming home. I was in the ninth grade then."

She said, "Yes."

I asked her, "Do you remember me saying I hated him and then running up the stairs."

She said, "Yes, but I just thought maybe that was because you two had been arguing or something."

I told her, "No, I really hated him, even though you always taught us not to have hatred toward one another."

I then went on to tell her about that Fourth of July, at that breathing house Daddy left us in. As she sat there trying to remember, the story walked up my throat, onto my tongue, and right out into the atmosphere.

See, my daddy brothers had been out in the backyard, where the raspberry bushes grew and no walls breathed. They were out there, popping firecrackers in soda pop bottles, watching them explode. I was in my room, planning things in my mind. I had heard Daddy Chaz out there laughing. Man, he seemed to be having a great time, out of juvy and all. So, I tiptoed down the steps, careful not to lean on the walls, and went out of the forbidden front door. I then snuck around the right side of the house. When I seemed close enough and could detect the direction his voice was coming from, The Mean Part jumped out and ran fast as lightning toward him. She punched him dead in his right eye. Then she opened the back door and ran, ran right up into your room.

"Remember, Mama, that night I rushed in and hid under your bed, and you caught Chaz at the door, making a border so he couldn't get in after me? Remember him hollerin' that I hit him?" But no one knew, not at that time, that it was The Mean Part. She was strong that night. She had been waiting all day, since he got home from juvy, to get him back.

Mama said, "Yes, but you and your brothers were always horseplayin'. But I remember asking you what was wrong and all you said was, 'Nothing, nothing other than, I don't like him sometimes.'"

There comes a time in a person's life when they have to make a conscious choice, whether to love or to hate. Mine, at the time, was to hate. But the flip side of that choice is the wear and tear it can have on the mind and body. People say God can heal all things. So I tried Him. I found great power in Him with faith. There is actual power to move mountains, mountains such as the ones I needed to move, so forgiving could take place. I didn't know how to do this. I needed something more powerful.

Therapy was good, it served its purpose, but something more powerful was needed to set the little girls inside me at peace, to reach down into the depths of my soul, so I could for-give my brother. I didn't think I'd ever be ready to do such a thing. The thing seemed so big, too big for me. But nothing is too big for God, and even though I couldn't see it, God was steppin' in. He stepped in as soon as Mama sat down in my living room.

Now, if there is one thing a mother has, it is love for her children. Mama was quiet for a while, but not long enough to lose me again.

She said, "Well, what can I say?"

I told her, "Nothing, but this was the reason I stayed away so long. I was going through things."

Of course, she followed with the whole "I could've helped you" discourse, but that was a given. I don't know how she would've helped, I'll never know because I separated myself from her and my brothers for six years. After the jail incident, she was forced to stay away and I just cuddled up in the com-fort of my temporary insanity.

Mama says I was never crazy. Maybe I wasn't, but I was sick. I know that much. I told her about my multiple person-alities, and for some reason, she understood completely. But she wanted to be assured some kind of way that they wouldn't escape somehow. I could not make that promise to her. I was still learning about them myself. Elaine and I cre-ated a place for them. The dollhouse with the white fence, the one I had when I was little, with the perfect family. That was their place. We stored all seven of them in there. That seemed to work for me. It also seemed to work that I was learning how to tell what triggered them, and when the dangerous one was close to escaping her glass walls.

Telling Mama about Daddy Chaz was where I needed to start. I knew she was going to have me sit down and talk with my other brothers in my own time. But she told me Daddy Bubba was fed up with missing me. He just kinda kept on going with his life. He got married and had a baby, even had a job right here in Washington State where I was. She told me I should really talk to him. But from my perspective, it was easier to just keep them out all together, although that was not realistic. We were, after all, a family.

My daughter had more family out there than me and my seven counterparts. She deserved more. I let Mama know I was still afraid that nobody would believe me. She told me not to worry about that, that she would be there.

She said, "I'll be there, and for every moment afterwards."

I still had to think about it all. Mama went back to Oregon after the weekend was over. Seeing her go was like eating the last piece of chocolate cake. Funny how much a part of our mothers we actually are.

Mama's stay was good. It was needed and it let me know a lot about her. That big heart of hers. I was hoping it was hereditary because I sure was gonna need it to face my daddy brothers. But I wasn't going to worry about all that just yet. I was still caught up in things; and work, along with school and my daughter, were a lot to balance.

At the time I started to reach out to my family, I was also working for a small family-owned newspaper. All I ever wanted to do since I could move my hands was write. I had already received my associate's degree in Journalism. This job seemed to be all right. The insurance was helping me to pay for my visits to Elaine, the owner seemed nice, and he, Homer, along with his wife, Penelope, seemed to care about me. She was always critical of me, though, trying to get me to do better. But Homer liked me a lot. I liked him, too, because I saw bits and pieces of the father I desired in him.

He would take me to his sales presentations, business functions, and he gave me fun and exciting tasks to do. He spent time talking to me about business, and how things should go, and how people are. I was already with the newspaper going on four years, through all my yucky stuff, too. But they didn't know much about that. I mean his wife knew and so did he, about the Daddy Chaz stuff, but it was all surface, I never got into detail. The key to them was that I was responsible, full of eagerness and life. I wanted to write. I wanted to work. I wanted to finish my bachelor's degree and raise my little girl with some dignity.

I loved the two of them, Homer and Penelope, because in

my eyesight they were somewhat perfect. They seemed to have that family I desired. But the funny thing is all that glitters is not gold. Yes, they were wealthy; they owned a newspaper, for goodness sake! The owner let me be in charge of a lot of things, too, and I liked that; I needed that. It made me feel big. I loved things that made me feel big. He never called me by my first named either, always by my last name, always. I guess that almost made me one of the guys.

Although Sookie was a good name, calling me by my last name kinda connected me to my daddy. And although my daddy was a flop, I still loved him. Despite Veronica, the lady he left my mama for, I still found it in my soul to love him. Now, since I knew I could do this, I also knew somewhere in me I could maybe love Daddy Chaz. But man, it sure seemed as if it would be a cold, cold day somewhere on a hot planet before I did.

*Now, Sookie kept going on about the business of living. She loved her job, school was going well, and she stopped seeing her daughter as if her daughter was her. She started to love Shuga for herself. This, in itself, was a miracle because The Mean Part had it in for that little girl, trying to drown her and all. Shoot, sometimes she'd lock Sookie up in a room, make her say she was never comin' out, just so Shuga would cry. I know there are angels because it's as if Sookie's daugh-*

ter had a sixth sense and knew her mama was ill with hurt. She kept loving her anyway.

I remember this one time Sookie came home. It was her graduation actually. She had been away from her mama for a long time by now. The guy thing, well, that's what triggered her. She was seeing this guy. He went with her to her graduation at the university, and don't let me forget to tell you it was her birthday, too. Well, he was acting real funny. Sookie wanted him to do something with her that day, stay with her so she wouldn't be lonely and all, and have one of them little girls inside her jump out and go boo! But after she walked across the stage and got her diploma and took a few pictures, on the way to the car he said he had to go.

Why on that special day? He just had to leave. This tore Sookie up, not so much that he had to go and wouldn't stay no matter how much she begged, but that she shut her mama out of this special day, and her mama always celebrated her birthday with her, not to mention she just graduated! Shoot, she shut Daddy Bubba out, too. She couldn't bring herself to call them, she was too busy running, trying to get well all by herself. Well, she managed to drive herself home that day. But as she was driving, that Mean Part broke those glass walls down, and Moan, the one who weeps everywhere, just started crying, and the other one, Blue, she got out of that box! Man, three of these raging little girls out all at once, not to mention one of The Twins, the Suicide Part, the one with the noose around her neck, she was free, too! Sookie was angry! She just got angry, a real special day and the dirty girl was all alone!

She ran up the stairs, leaving her daughter to tag along alone, and started yelling, cussing, hitting herself. It was too late to put them girls into the dollhouse; they had all gotten out. The Suicide Part had Sookie call up this guy and tell him she was gonna kill herself if he didn't come over! Imagine that! But this guy didn't care. There was no sex in it for him. Sookie was too shook up, so he told her, "Go right ahead and kill yourself." She hung up the phone and started hittin' on herself. Then she went to the hallway, where she hung her sheets that she painted these images of Daddy Chaz on, and she started painting him again, all the time just cussin'.

Well Shuga just backed off and kept asking Sookie what was wrong, but Sookie couldn't talk. Once she got those eyes onto the sheet, using black chalk, she went to the living room and got behind the futon couch, crouched down real low, and curled herself up in a ball. Sookie was trying to bust out 'cause she knew she needed to take care of Shuga, but man, if those little girls were not strong! They started beating on Sookie, punching her in the eyes and pinching at her skin. Sookie was bruised up by evening.

That's when she moved—in the evening. She needed help;

*she needed to put the little girls back. Where on earth was The Mommy Part, the one who could really help? I don't know what it was that shook Sookie back to reality, maybe it was one of her mama's prayers, from one of those long nights she spent on her knees. Maybe her mama was on her knees praying for her right then, at the moment those little girls were acting out.*

*She managed to get up and wipe her tears. She managed to get to the kitchen and cook dinner for her daughter and put her to bed. She managed to get into bed herself and let Moan do what she does best—weep. Blue got back into the box, it was too cold for her out there, and The Mean Part needed to be spanked, but since that couldn't happen, she stayed loose, loose until Sookie could get to Elaine.*

*Elaine wanted to know what happened. Sookie just went on to tell her how this guy doesn't love her, and she wanted him to love her so bad. Elaine kept telling her she needed to love herself first. But in Sookie's mind, there was nothing to love, it was all used up, all pissed on by Daddy Chaz. Shoot!*

I liked working for the newspaper. I liked the scholarships I won through working with them and their association with various family publishers. I just knew after getting my degree in English from the university and all, I'd be working for them a lifetime. How often is it someone knows where they're gonna be for the rest of their life? Well, I did.

Homer, the owner, offered me a trip to Disneyland once. He asked if I wanted to go and cover the opening of Toontown. I was excited with the idea of the whole thing. I said yes, and found someone to watch my daughter while I went. At that point, this man was everything to me, from a role model, to a mentor, to a father figure, to someone I thought I could love with all my heart.

He told me that I'd have to wear some other lady's nametag, which was okay with me. The other point was that I would have to fly out from Oregon. So what, a three-hour drive would do me good. I went. I met him at the Oregon office; and his brother, Jentry, drove us to the airport. We just chitchatted on the way there. It was very hot when we got off the plane and I knew my flannel Washington wear was going to have to be changed. This was my first real assignment that took me out of my element. I was big. I felt good. I felt normal and had no signs of the little girls coming out of their places in the dollhouse. Elaine and I went step by step over where each of the little girls would be, so I could function accordingly.

My room had a chocolate Mickey Mouse house in it. I vowed to myself never to eat it. It also had a red and white baseball cap that read Toontown, and if you flipped the lid of the hat, a pop-up cartoon town would appear. I always loved stuff that popped-up out of books. Pop-up books.

*Now, here is Sookie. Her eyes wide open with excitement, even in her early twenties. The chance to go to Disneyland made her happy, very happy and standing with Eyeore, seeing Minnie and Goofy.*

*Sookie, at some point though, let her guard down. The Mommy Part was sleepin', so it got right by her. The boss man she worked for had been really close to Sookie. After the second day of events he told her to come to his room after she came in from going out with some of the other young reporters who were there. She said, "Yes." Why not? He wanted to talk, to go over things, see what she had in mind to write.*

*Well, Sookie came back to the hotel about one in the morning. She called his room to let him know she made it back safely, and, lo and behold, he still wanted her to come down to his room! She checked herself over and trotted down the hall. The Mommy Part was still asleep. After all, what would a little girl be doing up so late anyway?*

*He opened the door and Sookie walked in. He told her to have a seat. The bed was really the only place to sit 'cause he had stuff in the chairs. As he talked to her, he took off his shirt 'cause I guess he was getting ready for bed. But this shook Sookie up some and she just stared at him. He saw her staring. The little girls started to wake up 'cause, see, they knew a man was around, and he was around at the wrong time.*

He looked at Sookie with those small, beady, brown eyes and asked her straight to her face if she liked him.

She said, "Yes."

Then he said it again, "Do you like me? You want to sleep with me, don't you?"

Her heart hit her back. I mean it almost broke through her vertebrae. Well, Sookie froze up. She couldn't move. Ice grew somewhere between her mind and her heart. See, the mind would've told her something wasn't right and the heart would've let her know something didn't feel right. But there was nothing but icicles there. Sookie told him, "Yes." You know, about the sex part. What was she to say? Maybe she would've lost her job and that couldn't happen, not with a little girl to support, therapy, and all the other stuff she had to pay for.

He was different from Daddy Chaz; he was slower, had groomed her, gained her trust and all. But he still went in for the kill. As he mounted her, somehow Moan came out, and since all she could see was his old, wrinkled back, she wept quietly so she would not get caught. Sure, Sookie went back to her room that night. She tried to wash the hell off of her body. When it was red and sore, and she realized soap could not get into her intestines, so she stopped. She stopped and flew back home in silence. Silence.

Silence can kill you if you're not careful. In my early twenties,

Daddy Chaz was off doing his own thing, no longer haunting me; yet he was still raging in me. Silence began to eat at me 'cause this boss man of mine told me that the night in that hotel was to be our little secret; nobody was to know. At night I'd hear his voice, I'd hear nobody has to know, nobody!

I'd be darned if I'd go to my grave with this man's voice. I had enough voices in my head already. The Mommy Part stepped out and the next time we saw Elaine, we told her, we told her everything. Turned out this boss man, who I had good love for, who was grooming me, took me out of my element just so he could sleep with me. He knew my head was not strong, he knew someone had preyed on me before. He had his turn. Well, I was gonna get mine!

Elaine kept telling me I had a certain amount of time to think, to report this type of rape. But you know what I wanted to do most? I wanted to tell. I wanted to let the secret out. I didn't want to hold it in. I didn't want to slowly let it rip my mind up, and in turn, watch my body split into more people. I wanted out—freedom. I knew this might mean my job. But I had to do it.

I wanted to tell his wife. I wanted to tell his rich, pretty wife, who criticized me and tried to help me grow as a writer. I wanted her to know her husband had sex with me and seven helpless little girls. I was too afraid to say "no" to him at the time. I was just too afraid.

I had a night job at the time, too, so I decided to call his wife when I was on shift. When she picked up the phone, I told her I had something to tell her. But please, let me first tell you how he fell apart once I told him I was gonna tell his wife what happened. He offered me more on the job, he pleaded for me, please not to, and he even asked me why I had to. I told him I was tired of keeping secrets; I didn't have enough room for them. What happened in California was wrong and it shouldn't have happened. He called me over and over again until I just had to stop answering the phone. Elaine says I should've saved the messages, but I didn't think about it at the time.

When his wife picked up the phone that day, I just came right out and said it, and not with a lot of carefulness the way I did when I told Mama about Daddy Chaz. See, this boss man was not her son. Anyway, figure this out. All his wife asked me was, "Did you like it?"

Did I like it?

I told her, "No!"

I didn't get fired from the job. It's as if in some odd way they wanted me to stay, but I never went back, not after that. I emptied my desk, shut down my computer and never went back. I had told and that's all I wanted to do. I didn't want any more men, any more people who pretended they loved me to dump on me anymore. It was time for a change.

# *Six*

---

*Will the real Sookie please stand up?*

Man, living with these little girls I rescued from those walls is making me tired. I keep trying to separate myself from them, but it seems like the harder I try, the more they try to act out. I understand they want love, they want freedom, they want a deliverance of some type; but the last time I checked, I was no superhero.

It can be one thing waking up one day feeling yourself feeling okay, feeling like everything is all together. It is another and a scary thing waking up and some kid is poppin' out, jumpin' on your bed. Getting to know the different girls inside of me as I got older was a necessity. It was the only way I could get any kind of grasp on how to help them, how to help myself and put them back into the doll house.

My centerpiece was my praying mama, though. Although she didn't know all of them, she knew some of the stronger ones, the ones who were so confused, they tried to shake me to my grave. I call her my centerpiece because when you're going through it, I believe there is something unseen that helps you make it, if you're determined enough. No, I'm not talking about those ghosts from that house, but something unseen, beautiful, and really powerful. Mama prayed for me the entire time I was away. She was taking part in the power God can give someone through prayer.

See, when you're aching inside and crying in the dark, there has to be something lighter around you, something with force that takes your pain elsewhere and lifts you up to a higher place, a place that allows you to make it through the next day. There is only one force powerful like that: *God*.

I began to believe this more and more because I know the devil doesn't have the power to know what someone is thinking, just like he does not have the power to create life. I spent a lot of nights crying and talking to myself in my mind. I needed to do that so I could think clearly.

Even though I was still struggling and sleeping around with all sorts of guys, trying to fight my own demons, I still prayed like Mama told me to. I'd ask God for things and to help me through. As time went on, I joined a church. It was a small Baptist church, like the one Mama used to go to back east in Washington, D.C. It was full of black folk, and they could sang! Not sing, but *sang*! I loved it because it reminded me of home, the sweet part of home, before Oregon, before that house.

So I did go into this church with expectations. I expected that I would gain something, something that would help me face the fear I had been running from. These folks didn't know me, they didn't know anything about me and my little girls. All they saw was what I wanted them to see. God saw the rest. I would stand up and clap and imagine Mama right beside me, singing the way she did at her church on Tenth Street in Washington, D.C.

The imagining gave me the courage to stand. My daughter would start off sitting, but soon enough she'd join me and try to catch the beat with her small, caramel candy-colored hands. When time came to sit and listen, I did just that, the whole time looking for God's answers in what the preacher man was saying. I went up for altar call, too. I felt like there was strength in a thing like this. Why, all those people gathered together holding hands. I didn't think I could be part of something like this after all the cult trickery. But I was.

See, since I had been tricked before, I had to make sure I went to a place that was familiar, and childhood things are always familiar. They have a way of making you feel safe. I remember going to church with Mama. I remember her chasing me around trying to get me to put a dress on my tomboy legs. And I remember sitting there the whole time waiting to get out, so I could run and play like my daddy brothers. The funny thing is, though, if she couldn't catch them, she always made sure to catch me.

There's something about the discipline of going to church that sticks with you, so that's what I looked for when I got up the courage to go back to church. The place was small, and there sure was no one in there predicting the future and hollerin' at everyone, taking everyone's money along with their belief. It was just plain folks, coming together, singing, listening, and holding hands. Since Mama was still in Oregon and I was still toiling with the idea of seeing my daddy brothers, well, Daddy Bubba in particular, I just imagined her there with me. It gave me the strength to go back every Sunday. And, well, those Sundays were working on me, the little girls inside me, and my soul.

Mama called. She wanted to know in a nutshell if I was ready to see Daddy Bubba. I knew he was angry with me, but how was I gonna make sense out of all my running? Mama said she'd be right there with me to serve as some sort of cushion. Sometimes angry folks seem as though they can always hear their mama, even if they can't hear anything else. I told her I'd go.

She came up from Oregon and we went over to Daddy Bubba's house. He moved to Washington after his time in the U.S. Navy. He was married now, as I said earlier, and man, had he changed. He still was light-skinned the way I remembered him, just older in the face, experienced. I sat on the couch in his somewhat blank house; I figured it was new. I waited.

He sat across from me, waiting for an explanation as to why the family should trust me anymore, why they should let me be a part of their world, their happiness, after I shut the doors on them. I could not bring up The Mean Part, or any of the little girls inside of me, I had to just move on and speak, somehow. Mama told him I've changed. I told him I've changed. I told him Daddy Chaz hurt me something awful, but he just went on and on about why I never said anything to anybody.

Family is strange sometimes. In a way, I don't think he believed me. It was like my being molested just passed right by him. But that didn't really matter to me at the time. Mama's belief was most important. It seemed as though I couldn't say sorry enough, it seems as though I was the dirty bad girl all over again. I hated that. I felt my head throbbing, and I felt the glass walls begin to shake inside the dollhouse where The Mean Part was. I had to go. I had to end this conversation and go.

Things didn't get solved right away, but it was a start. I think. I wondered a lot about why I felt like I had to prove myself to Daddy Bubba, when I was the one who got hurt, whose insides were torn up. It's not something that can be brushed away so easily, the fact that your flesh and blood raped you. But I think he thought it could be, put in a box because a part of me just knew he didn't believe me. He wanted me to get over it and just be a family, forgive.

If it was that easy . . .

I stayed away a little while longer. I made sure I talked with Mama more than less. I kept going to that small church where the people seemed alright and I could sing and listen for God to move. Dating for me was alright. I seemed to be looking for my daddy less and less, and looking for stability more and more. The toughest thing for me to learn, though, was that sex was not going to gain that stability for me. From doggie style to anyway they wanted it . . . sex was not the answer.

I began to think a lot about fornication and then marriage. I began to think what would happen if I actually waited and began to pray more for God to send me a husband. *Husband*! What a joke that sounded like. I remember this one guy telling me to my face no one would ever want to marry me. I actually believed him for a long time because I knew I was used up and already had a kid. But I decided to try—why not try—abstinence. I tried just about everything else, looking for happiness, looking for a sense of completeness.

This was hard at first. I slipped, and slipped, and slipped. But one day I looked at Shuga and it was final. If she was seeing me do all this, if she was seeing me do all this sleeping around, if she was seeing me not love myself, what kind of woman was that going to make her? I had to get better, I had to move on in a way, like Daddy Bubba mentioned.

It got so that my soul got hungry for more and more preaching, more singing. So I joined the choir and kept my little girls in their separate places for quite some time. God was doing something in me and as I slept at night, other things came to me in my sleep. Seems like these other things that crept around my conscious were trying to counter what God was trying to do and they came slowly, in dreams I wanted to push off a cliff. Daddy Chaz was back again.

I had another dream. I dreamed he died. I didn't cry. He died from a crack overdose. He was thin, frail, and breakable. I felt like God had freed me. Everyone was crying, 'specially Mama, even my daddy brothers, but not me. I did not shed one tear.

"Should I feel guilty for this?" I asked myself. I couldn't answer. It didn't feel right to answer this question. People might think I'm crazy. But the answer, regardless of them out there, is I didn't. I did not feel guilty for not shedding any tears. Who cares that it was a dream? Who cares that he was really still alive? The point is I didn't cry. I sat there amongst everyone in their black and smiled inside. I smiled big, like I was at the fair with my mama and Ronald McDonald, eating an ice cream cone at the Washington monument. He was dead. I was free.

*Now, Sookie was too close to quittin'. She wanted to see herself through this, but nightmares can take a toll. Daddy Chaz started stomping around in her mind, threatening her, making her wake up with salty tears. He started making her think someone was behind her all the time, looking for her.*

*In these dreams, though, she'd begin to run. It wasn't like before when she was always smaller and had fear burning in the pit of her stomach. Yeah, she began to run away from him. Sometimes she'd wake up so tired that she just wanted to sleep all day, but only in the daylight could she rest, never in the night. What got real good about these dreams, though, is that Sookie began hearing other things in her mind. Daddy Chaz would come at her and she'd say a scripture she heard in church to him and he would either stop in his tracks or disappear for a while.*

*Sometimes when she slept, she heard them church songs playing real loud in her mind, and Daddy Chaz would just crack up, crumble right there into a million pieces like one of them complicated jigsaw puzzles. But Sookie still didn't like these dreams. She wanted to sleep. All she wanted was sleep. She began to leave work early. Before getting her daughter Shuga from daycare, she'd go down to the water's side and sleep, listening to the waves. She'd set the alarm on her watch so she wouldn't stay past the closing time of the day-care center. She also began to fight harder; Sookie began to pray more, 'cause there was something to these scriptures and songs coming into her mind at the moments she was scared the most.*

I began to remember Daddy Chaz and some of the things he told Mama in that house. I remember the time he told her he saw the devil standing right there at the foot of his bed. I knew Daddy Chaz was not born the way he was. Something happened. Something had to happen to him. But what? What was so awful?

I remember the times Elaine had told me Daddy Chaz's behavior was a learned behavior; kids don't just grow up to hurt others. I hated hearing that at the time, but now I wanted to know. I wanted Daddy Chaz to tell me to my face and in front of the family that he had molested me. I wanted to get inside the maze of his mind and let him tell me what happened to him. But I didn't know if I could do all this.

Parts of me didn't want to forgive him, but look at Christ.

Really, this was a man who didn't have to get up on that cross and forgive all our sins, even the cruelty of sins like murder and rape, but he did! He took nails in his hands and feet, and had his side pierced, then just up and died to teach us all! We stink. We're a stinky people with all our skeletons. But he loved us enough to give us a second chance. Could I do this? Could I face Daddy Chaz and try to see that the ugly in him was just that, ugly. Something that entered him and was not born in him.

Ugly had done enough to me by separating my family. How many more Christmases was my daughter gonna miss being with her grandma on account of my running? How many more years was Daddy Bubba gonna keep changing and becoming more of a family man with me not being there to see just how much unlike Daddy he was? How much longer was ugly gonna be allowed to creep around in my sleep because Daddy Chaz was still the same in my mind. He was someone bigger than me, someone over top of me, making me bleed.

Mama called. I told her what I had been thinking about. And she opened up some untold truths about Daddy Chaz. I believe they helped me. They helped me make a decision that needed to be made in order to stop ugly. See, all that time I was away, all that time I had been running, Daddy Chaz had been running, too. Seems as though he was trying to run from himself, and it's a sad thing when a man tries to run from himself because what he's actually trying to do is kill himself.

Mama told me he had been using crack. She had trouble digesting this herself, but after she found out what happened to me, she did go to him and ask him if he did it. He told her, "No," right to her face. But mamas have this way of just knowing their children and knowing when they lie.

There was a time she made us all line up to see who stole her wallet. She looked the four of us dead in the eye and asked us all. It was Daddy Chaz who looked down, who fidgeted. She knew he was lying, but couldn't do much more then. But now, she just told him to get out, to get out of her house. She knew he lied about me. He left, but he left with his head beneath his tail. She said she had heard that he had been using crack, so she went to look for him downtown. He was downtown. He was behind a Burger King eating out of the garbage.

Oh yes, she wanted to run to her son. He was still her son, but when she called out to him, he didn't even recognize her. See, the same amount of time I was keeping my secrets and the six years I ran and shut everyone out, and split into seven different people, he was trying to destroy himself. He tried continually committing crimes. He tried beatin' ugly out of the girls he dated. He tried weed, but it was too weak, not strong enough to push his realities away. It just wasn't strong enough.

I knew a large part of him was still missing Daddy, 'cause Daddy's leaving had a strong effect on all of us. Men don't realize how strong their presence, as a father, is until they bury one of their children who died in the process of looking for them.

Daddy Chaz was close to death, and Daddy didn't even know. He didn't even know any of the roads our lives took after he left Mama for Snow White because he never called to check up on us. He never came to see us. He never even called to wish us happy birthday, Merry Christmas, or just to say a simple hello, how are you? He just up and left and seemed not to care. And when a child thinks their parents don't care, after falling in love with them, it breaks them up inside. Daddy Chaz was all broke up, still. In this way, we were alike. And I never imagined I could be, in any way, like the person who murdered my insides. But Daddy's leaving broke me up, too.

Daddy Chaz used crack for a while. He even got his lady friend to join in. But this in no way saved him. It did not save him from the lie he told to Mama's face. I know this is true because God opened a doorway that brought us all together.

It happened to be on Easter. Imagine that. Well, Mama

had done her usual cooking, with smell-goods dripping from the walls of her new house. It was a relief not to see them walls move. Once everyone had eaten and began to sit around and talk, she called Daddy Chaz on the telephone. He was staying with his lady friend, the one he loved so much that he shared his desire for crack with her. He came over, but he didn't know I was there. But I knew he was coming. For once, I had the upper hand and Mama had given it to me by making sure none of this would happen unless I was ready. I had prayed myself up; I was ready. When he came though, I went upstairs and went into the bedroom. Mama came after me, looked me in the eyes to make sure she was seeing just me. I was okay. The Mean Part was shaking real bad, though. I was trying to keep her still, for Mama's and my sake. I made it down the stairs with Mama holding my hands, and all the hands of the little girls. Deep breath.

Daddy Chaz was here, on the midnight blue couch at Mama's, with his lady friend. They didn't seem high. They seemed downright normal to me. He glanced up and said, "Hi." I don't know if I said "hi" back; I was too busy listening to my heartbeat. Mama called Daddy Bubba, and Daddy Tee. They came with their wives. We all went down to the basement since the kids were outside playing. Daddy Chaz kept asking, what's going on, what's the big secret? My mind was screaming, what's the big secret? If God hadn't been in my soul, maybe I would've cursed him in front of everybody or grabbed one of those knives used to cut the turkey and stabbed him real good in his private parts.

Once we got down there, nobody sat. Nobody. Mama told Daddy Chaz she was only gonna ask him once, and he better not lie this time. She held my hand and asked him in front of everyone, did he ever touch me. He said, "Yes."

Yes! He said it right to my mama's face. Yes, he did touch me. I turned and all the little girls jumped out at once. I hit the wall with my fist and ran up the stairs. I was twenty, eighteen, twelve, eleven, ten, nine, eight, seven, six years old! I made it out the front door with Mama on my trail. She had fallen up the steps trying to catch me, but somehow caught up to me. Then the voice of my daughter broke through and halted my departure. I was halfway down the block by then.

When Mama grabbed me, I told her, "I'm gonna throw up!"

She told me, "Throw up then, throw up!"

I felt so sick, but looking into those brown eyes of hers steadied me something good. The little girls stopped, too. They had no real place to go but back into their rooms. It was my turn to really save them, my turn to be their night light in the dark. Mama took my hands, pulled me close and held me. She let me cry into her. Daddy Bubba came, but I don't think he ever really knew what was going on. Why Mama was hugging all seven of them little girls, including me, with just the two arms God gave her.

I fell in love with her all over again. She asked me, "Are you okay to go back?"

I told her, "Yes," and we walked slowly, but if Daddy Chaz wasn't trying to leave! It was Daddy Bubba who pulled him off to the side, telling him it's time we all stopped running.

He tried to say, "Maybe it's better if I leave."

Mama chimed in and said, "No, we're all going in."

And ugly was about to get shot in the private parts.

*Sookie, if she wasn't a hero before, she was one then. She once wrote a story about being a superhero. It went this way.*

My mama used to tell me if I quit using so many "I's" in my stories, and not write about myself so much, my work would be better. She would tell me to distance myself from the material. I listened to her but in my mind I kept thinking, I write what I know, and what I know are things that happened to me. She would tell me if I kept using so many I's, it would seem like I was trying to glorify myself; the material would be too vain. Well, I don't know how much Mama knows about writing. After all, she's a registered nurse. She went to school, with four children and worked two jobs until she graduated with that nursing degree.

She called herself the fly in the buttermilk. This was because she says she was the only black in her class during that time. She said the only other black girl dropped out because things got too tough. Mama made a lot of friends during her time there. And color wasn't an issue. Everybody was trying for the same thing. They wanted to finish, so they could move on and nurse other folk.

Mama was never scared of blood, like me. Boy, with three daddy brothers I was always up in trees, on dirt bikes, and in the mud. One time I was playing Wonder Woman and my best friend, Emma, was Dyna Girl. See, I was always the superhero and Emma was my sidekick. My daddy brothers never settled for being Robin, so neither did I. They were always hot shots, like Batman or Conan.

Anyway, we were climbing the side of the garage in the backyard of the house where I grew up, and the window was broken out. Emma went up first, since she was smaller, and being the superhero, I could catch her if she fell. On my way up, my knee swung right into a nail, and it hit me like a dagger. I jumped down, all the time hearing my daddy brothers' voices in my head. They were telling me not to cry, to fight the pain! I was biting my lower lip as tears burned the rim of my eyes. Emma came down and called Daddy Tee out of the house.

He came out and when his face almost turned blue, I

almost fainted. He told me not to look down at it, and to grab onto him to help me fight the pain. I bit into his shoulder instead. We got inside the house and into the TV room. Willie Wonka and the Chocolate Factory was concluding. He laid me down and called Mama. It was finals week for her. She told him to lay me down on the floor and prop my legs up against the wall, this was to keep the blood from draining out my knee too fast. She said she'd be home soon.

From the view down on the floor, I could see my knee. I asked Daddy Tee what were those little white balls inside my knee. He told me he thinks they are my white blood cells. By this time, Wonder Girl was gone. It was just me and my bro. He just watched me and my blood cells. Then I heard the back door close. Daddy Bubba had come in. He looked at me, at my knee, then back at me. He asked me how did it feel looking at the ceiling? He then went on to make faces at me, bubbling out his cheeks and all. I laughed. I was also glad we weren't back east, where a roach could've fell off the ceiling and into my face.

Mama seemed like she would never come home, but she made it and we rushed to the hospital. Daddy Bubba rode with us, making faces along the way. He was a great brother to have around when white things were rolling around in your knee. I ended up getting stitches. Mama tucked me in that night and told me how she wished I would stop climbing all them trees and be the lady girl she knew I could be. But I enjoyed wearing jeans and jumping off of things.

The next day, I went back to play with Emma. I had to lay low since I couldn't climb. Later that day, we went on to egg the neighbor's house, and I even let Emma be the superhero. It was only fair. Everyone should know what it feels like to be me.

*Now, that was it. Sookie wrote that superhero story. And she did share the stardom with Emma. But what's different now is Sookie is all grown up, still lovin' them jeans. But to face Daddy Chaz she had to be Wonder Woman, Dyna Girl, and Superman. She couldn't share this with nobody. She was always a good dreamer; it kept her alive. But now it was the real deal. Sookie was breaking tradition; she was tellin', lettin' the whole secret out for all the world to breathe and gasp at.*

Daddy Chaz sat on the ottoman to our great-grandma's rocking chair. It was one of the precious things Mama came back with after she went to her grandmother's funeral. To me, he was not worthy enough to sit on it. Mama went on to ask him why he molested me, and the cat opened his mouth! He said it was because of Daddy. He was angry with Daddy, because Daddy hurt him, see. He said since I seemed to be the closest thing to Daddy, after he left, he decided to go after me. And he even went on. He pulled in his weed and his drug using, saying sometimes he was just high, and didn't even remember the things he did to me. But he was conscious enough to remember them this time, as Mama asked him, as Daddy Bubba asked him, as Daddy Tee asked him. The fool. What an excuse!

# *Seven*

---

Mama said she was sure glad I found myself, and then made a small comment about how long it took. Yes, I admit it took me a long time to get those little girls in a somewhat safe place, then to trust God and confront my fear of Daddy Chaz. The big deal to me, though, was that it seemed as if God didn't leave any of my requests unanswered. Not like it was some sort of "do whatever I say" kinda thing, but it was real. I mean, I got on my knees, even when I wasn't sure of how I was living, and asked for help.

I know people say God is the healer of all things, but it just hit home for me. 'Cause it was like He used Elaine and all her doctor knowledge, along with those therapy sessions I thought would never end, and made everything work together for His good. Like in Romans 8:28. Now this, to me, is special because I could not see the good in some of this, just the need.

Seeing Daddy Chaz on Easter was just the beginning. The wounds that were bleeding and open inside of me were now being cleansed and covered with soft gauze bandages. They were even complete with Neosporin ointment. And it was on account of God, Mama, Elaine, and me, just being eager enough to make a change.

When I was little, when we still stayed in that house with those breathing walls, Mama used to take me on long rides with her. They were usually to go see one of her patients that lived out on the outskirts of town. But some days we'd see a rainbow, and if Mama got the urge she'd say, let's drive to the end of it! My heart would jump, and I was sure we'd never go back home again. No more Daddy Chaz, ever.

But it never went that way. We would drive and drive and drive. We'd go around curves, hit dead ends, old neighbor-hoods. Then we'd make it out to where the cows were, the horses, and then the water. The water never seemed to end, but it did. And we never got to the rainbow. It would either disappear laughing at us, or we would disappear laughing at ourselves. So here I was, chasing after the rainbow, with belief that things can get better if I try. If I drive far enough, and push the gas hard enough, I will see the pot of gold. Facing Daddy Chaz was the start of reaching this sought-after gold.

Now, the real work was gonna start. I knew nightmares were gonna come back, based on the simple fact that I saw him face to face, and the mind has a way of blowing things up and making them bigger than they are. But this time, instead of just letting the nightmares come and bubble up inside of me, I reached for the phone and called Mama. We would talk. *We would pray.*

My life began to change. In that small church I was going to I met a young man. He was not loud and outlandish, like the men I was used to wasting my time with. Nor did he seem like a search for my daddy in any way. He was just quiet, set aside, and into what he was doing, praising God.

*Now, Sookie has to move on with this story here. Bring it to some sort of sweet closure. But, see, she can't do this until she tells y'all about all the important things. See, after being molested, raped, having them multiple personalities and all, folks don't expect you to get well. They don't expect you to go back and face your demons, much less your abuser. No, they expect you to hang yourself, or fade away into the darkness of silence, or even worse, become like those who hurt you.*

*But Sookie, she didn't and that's what I like about her. Man, she started putting two and two together, started loving her daughter Shuga, calling out to God, and praying, and things started happening! And it's very important folks don't see this as any sort of luck or magic, 'cause it wasn't. It all came together too nicely, too completely. Although she cried sometimes, and bucked, and kicked, it still came together.*

*Now, remember there was this guy who even told broken up ol' Sookie that nobody would ever want to marry her, 'cause she had a kid already and was all used up by everyone else? Well, even he gets proven wrong.*

*But the really great part is Sookie and Daddy Chaz. See, while Sookie is meeting this young man in the church and being wooed, Daddy Chaz is starting to feel the flux of his mama's praying. Yup, cracked out and all, he became part of this home for folks like him. This place had rules, too, and one of those rules was going to church, and the other was keeping the curfew. But if Daddy Chaz didn't give his life to Christ, too! Yup, he got down on those crusty knees of his and asked the Lord to forgive him, for all his muck. Boy, I knew this was gonna get Sookie, but how, I didn't know.*

Mama called me and told me Daddy Chaz was going to church, but more than that she told me he gave his life to Christ. I got quiet. What else could I do? Was I supposed to shout up and down for joy?

I wanted to cuss, to be honest. Salvation is great, really. But you must admit, it seems unfair that some folk get to have it. Who am I to say such a thing? But it does seem that way, 'cause we stink. With all our goof-ups and failures, we smell bad! I'm glad someone has a big enough heart, outside that of our own mothers, to love us this much.

It's real hard talking about all this with you all. I mean this is my story, my ugliness and beauty all wrapped up in these pages. And just when I feel like I made it a step further, my jaws get tight, my heart tries to shut up and close down; then something big happens, God steps in, and I find myself trying all the harder.

I listened to Mama as she said Daddy Chaz was now part of the same Christian family I was. What about the devil that came to the foot of his bed in that breathing house? Man. I hung up the phone.

*Now, they say that every time a soul comes to Christ the angels in heaven rejoice. Sookie didn't seem like she was rejoicing. With this newfound change in his life, I guess Daddy Chaz didn't feel like he needed to do any more explaining. He sat down at Mama's one night and told them all that he didn't need to say anything else, not even sorry, 'cause that's what Sookie was there waiting for again.*

*She figured, "Why not?" It was dinner, everyone was there. Now, have some compassion about the matter! But he didn't. Sookie even brought that new guy she was seeing home with her. Mama knew Sookie was hungry for a sincere apology, so she brought it up, but Daddy Chaz just put up them barriers again. Seemed like he became another person all at once.*

So what? You don't feel like you need to say anything. Is it that you are holier than thou now and don't need to say anything? I was hot! I didn't say these things to Daddy Chaz, but I was hot. My mind was thinking these thoughts. It was hard for me to sit at another family gathering and just watch him and everyone else.

Yes, I said hi.

Yes, I sat down to the table like everyone else.

Yes, I loved Mama, was willing to try, had Christ, too.

But gosh! This, to me, seemed insane! Daddy Bubba and Daddy Tee, joking, Daddy Chaz just a-talking and those little girls inside of me started to move, started to shake. Mama wasn't watching me, so she didn't see any of the signs.

I went up to the room and shut the door. After awhile, Mama noticed I was gone and came up. I started to cry. I had to tell her how hard this is. I told her, "I know I have Christ and so does he, and now we are all to be this happy family, but I still honestly feel like I hate him."

Mama sat close to me and told me, "It's okay." She said, "This thing is not going to go away over night. It's gonna take time, and nobody knows how much time it's gonna take but the good Lord Himself. This is a start."

*A start.* I had no idea I'd ever bring myself to such a place as "a start." None.

The ugliness of the past and the power of a present God seemed heavy to handle at first. I wanted to go back to my apartment, but I had my daughter and had driven a long way, so I stayed. To my surprise, when Mama and I came down the steps, Daddy Chaz had already left. My daddy brothers said he went to church. Kind of ironic, huh? Not really. God is that good and big, and ugly needed to be sent to hell because it had done enough. If only I could separate the ugly from my brother.

*Sookie eventually made it back to her home in Washington with her new friend. This guy was a gentleman, too. He never made a pass at her, not even after spending the weekend at her mama's house and all. They slept in separate rooms, and Sookie was just kinda drooling over this whole thing. She never had a guy just talk to her and not expect sex or anything. This made her whole task of trying to finally save what little she had left of herself easier.*

*Her daughter actually liked the guy, too, and this was a small miracle. See, Shuga didn't like any of those men that called on her mama in the wee hours of the night. She was small and couldn't voice herself much, but she knew deep inside she didn't like those men. But this guy she liked, and so it went.*

*Sookie and he began to see each other more, go to movies, parks, and take walks. They even went to church together and that was a big deal, see, 'cause small town church folk who are used to things going one way, if a bump arises, they talk. So Sookie and her man friend became the all-new "bump" after holding hands at the alter call. But I was proud of Sookie, and all her little girls inside, 'cause she didn't let the gossip by church folk run her off. And if she had any doubts, any at all, why, she'd call her mama up and talk to her about it.*

Color set aside, I needed a new church home. I needed more variety. Shuga wanted to be a part of more kids' activities, and the seventies, after all that protesting and standing up for our color, was over. There were mixed kids everywhere and God, I figured, is colorblind, anyway. He loves everybody.

So, I wanted to be more color blind in the way I worshipped. Besides, the small town church folks were starting to wear on me. I knew there had to be a bigger place of worship that would be more suited for my daughter and me. What I didn't know was that this guy friend of mine would be out looking for that new church home right along with me and my daughter. Shoot, he was raised in that church we met in. He preached in that church. There was no way he could leave it! But in the coolness of one evening, this guy asked me to marry him. Me! *Me!*

It was Sookie he loved. We had the chance to talk during the months we went out. After all, he wasn't jumping my bones, so we had to do something else with the time. He knew about all my mud and muck, all of it, and said he loved me anyway, wanted to spend the rest of his life with me, his friend.

After I called Mama and told her, even set a date, we ended up running off, eloping. No white gown, no puff and fuss, or millions of dollars spent on bridesmaids. We just took our virgin love and jumped in! Shuga was my flower girl, Daddy Bubba was actually a witness, along with his wife, and we did it, we got married. Mama was mad at first. She was mad that I didn't wait for or involve her. She wanted to know what the rush was, and so forth.

But there was no rush. I wasn't running from anything for once, I just wanted it, the happiness and his smile, all right then and there. I didn't want to wait until June or the next year, for that matter. If it was right, which we both felt it was, we would survive, no matter what. And I never met a man so in love with God.

I felt so good about myself. So changed. God heard me again, and I had waited for this. Even through my blemished and used up body, I waited for him and here I was, married now. This, to me, was the biggest separation from my daddy. I had moved on. I no longer had his last name. I still favored him with my looks, but the whole name thing seemed like a neat way to put closure on his never really being involved in our lives after he left Mama.

I was a "Mrs." now, a lady, a wife. Our honeymoon was no exotic trip to the Bahamas, but a quiet evening at home alone, followed by a nice breakfast. We enjoyed each other, and I was glad I was me. I was learning who I was, and not dealing with seven little people running loose all over the place, hurting folks. I almost liked myself, too.

# *Eight*

Now, my husband says being married is part of an upper class. This made me smile. He put up with my tomboyishness, jeans, and t-shirts. He didn't mind my nails being yea long, or my face just as it was, no fancy colors or runny make-up. He said he loved me just the way I was. It felt good to smile, to be adored.

For the first time in my life since leaving Mama's house, I was not going to have to work. I had my degrees and all, but he was going to work for the U.S. Navy and let me stay home with Shuga. He thought the two of us had lost enough time already.

At first, I was nervous about this, thought I really might go crazy. But it didn't turn out that way. Time was healing for Shuga and me. And for once in my life, I felt like I was getting to know my daughter for who she was. At first, I wanted to be mad at myself for ever trying to hurt her, but that would have taken too much time away from us. Instead I gave it to God, and worked on forgiving myself, hoping she would see the light in me and forgive me, too.

I knew she probably didn't remember much, but children are not stupid. We just make the mistake of underestimating them all the time. Going to the parks in the middle of the day, reading stories and not skipping the pages because I was tired and had to work the next day, waking up at ten and watching *Sesame Street*, this was nice, it was peace.

My husband got us into family housing in no time, and this gave us more space to grow into loving each other. At first, I was shaky, kinda thought the walls would breathe, but then I remembered, I *was* okay *now*.

I thought I should do something in honor of the little girls who once raged inside me full-time, in honor of facing Daddy Chaz and confronting him. So, I told my husband next time I go to Mama's house, I was gonna go by the house I grew up in and look in every single window, and then have a kind of ceremony, letting myself see just how much in the past all this ugly was. But I didn't know how much memory one house could hold.

The rain was pouring down the day we decided to go by *that house*. Everyone was home again, no holiday, just everyone wanting to get away from his or her own kingdoms and be embraced by Mama's. My husband and I kinda snuck away. I didn't really want anyone to know what I was doing.

When we got to the street the house was on, my heart started racing, it pounded my chest like big enormous drops of hail, the kind that comes out of nowhere. First, there is sun, then there is a cloud, then these big ice balls come and beat on your windowpane. Yup, hail. I parked the car right in front of the house. All I could do was look at it at first. It was empty. It seemed to always be empty after we moved out of it.

I approached the front porch and went to the house numbers and wiggled them. The number eight still came out of its place. I almost stole it and put it in my pocket, but I didn't; that would've been wrong and not what I was there for. As I glanced at the front door, I remembered the guy that came to take Mama out, Dirk. I let that scene run through my head. I let the punishment run through my head, and I let Daddy Chaz run through my head. I never saw the details in the floor of my room until that night. The black lines in the tile, my doll knocked over to my side. It was over; I was alive. I then walked down the steps and went around the side of the house, to the alleyway where I used to ride the bikes my brothers built for me with junky or stolen bike parts.

As I looked vertically up the side of the house, I could have sworn I saw blood droplets the size of the fruit inside a pomegranate. I took a deep breath in, my husband by my side. I looked in through the doorway that led down to the basement where ugly lived inside the cold cement room. I made myself look into that empty basement. *Empty. Nobody was in there.* I looked around, corner to corner, and then stepped back.

My eyes traveled upward to the bathroom window. The bathroom I had to crawl to, where an angel held me up and washed me clean from all the sticky stuff and blood tinge. I backed up again. My eyes then moved to the left and froze. I saw what was once my daddy brother's room. The window I was fixed on was the room where the devil stood at the foot of Daddy Chaz's bed. There were no curtains. It was *empty.*

But no, it couldn't be empty, he had to still be in that house somewhere, waiting for me; he was up there; I just knew it!

I wanted to break into the house, set it on fire, burn the walls up. Maybe if I was lucky, I could find a gasoline can, maybe in that dumb basement and then get him while he was sleeping. I'd pour it on him, then light it, and as Daddy Bubba would jokingly say, watch him go boom!

I backed up and took another deep breath. Tears began to burn the rim of my eyes. I let them.

I whispered, "There is no one there. There is no one there!"

As I blinked, I moved toward the backyard. Someone had cut the raspberry bushes down, the place where a praying mantis greeted the back of my hand and Daddy stood there smiling at me from the kitchen window.

It was one of my last memories of him being home. Other than this small change, the backyard was still the same. The garage window was still broken. I'm sure Wonder Woman was inside waiting for me.

I looked up to the kitchenette, where a million peas hit the ceiling and a thousand chicken livers were fed to the six-toed cat, Taurus. It was empty. The strange thing was, both doors were shut that would've allowed me to look into the dining or living room. That was all right for a while. I had to see them, though. My husband took me to the next window over and lifted me up. *Empty.* I took another deep breath, and as my feet hit the ground, it was time now to look into that empty, cold cellar.

I didn't know what I expected to see. I knew ugly was pissed at me by now, was probably waiting to jump me at the car. I looked into it. This was the only window with tiny metal bars all over it, as if to prevent whatever lived in there alone from ever escaping. It was full. Yes, full. I could still feel something there, inside. I moved back a little, it was strong, kind of raging.

I believe the spirit of incest was hibernating there, from the rain. I believe it ruled that house, kept anyone who tried to move in from staying there too long. I cried again. The tears didn't burn though; they just fell softly, blending in with the pitter-putter of raindrops.

I looked toward the driveway. Man, it seems as if this house was bigger than ever now. I saw the mint bushes and flower bushes I played mud pies with. I used to make tacos out of their leaves. I saw the corner where I made mud burgers and topped them with stones. I saw my bedroom window, with the same Z100 sticker still on it, and the roof. This was the same roof I climbed out on, trying to hide. I once smoked a cigarette out there; at least I thought I did.

My room. The curtains were gone. No longer pink. But a dull beige covering kept my eyes from going inside. But my heart said, it too was *empty*. I'm somewhat glad for the curtains, I may have gotten lost in the closet, which was not what I was there for.

The rest of the house was just plain *empty*. We, as children, were never allowed to play in the living room much, but do I remember that Christmas, the doll house, the pogo stick, the tenny-shoe skates, Daddy and Mama, a prayer plant safe on the table, leaves opened wide. I looked at my husband, who took my hands.

I told him I was not done yet. I had to bury the little girls. So, I dug a small hole and opened the chambers of my mind. I unhooked the lock on The Mean Part's glass door. She stepped out, shaking. I let Blue out of the box. Mona got off the couch and The Twins came from the playroom. The Mommy Part was in the kitchen, she walked out slowly, and Moan, she came from the backyard of the dollhouse and winked at me. To my surprise, she had no tears. I took my hands and placed them in the soil and then covered the girls up.

I figured one day I'd see them at the end of the rainbow, or up in heaven where my great-grandmama was, just as long as they were free from those walls, and safe in the arms of some archangel that guards this corner of the universe. With one intake of memory-filled air, I walked to the car and said, "Good-bye."

My eyes hit the front windows of the room where my Daddy Tee used to build model skeletons. Once he even felt the need to share and left one in my bed to say hello to me after I got out the shower one night. Instead, I screamed and ran to Mama's room. She went to his bedroom as if to punish him, but was really laughing, hitting a pillow instead, to make me think he was getting a spanking. It's funny now that I'm older. *Older.* That's what I am. And these are memories. *They cannot control me.*

I got into the car and we drove off somewhat slowly. The water tower still had the name of Daddy Bubba's gang, The Trojans, painted on it. It took me years to figure out what that name was implying. I smiled. I held my husband's hand because I had a lot of living to start doing now. But as the car went forward, it was as if I heard the doors of chambers closing, slamming, and voices yelling, wailing. I wondered if the house was falling down. But I didn't look back. That was not what I was there for.

# *Nine*

Dear Daddy,

I often think, "What would I say to you if I had the chance?" Would I scream in your ears, or would I just hug you? I sometimes think, "Is it worth it to even say anything?" But it is. Oh, it is. See, dealing with your leaving Mama took a long time. Because when you left, the walls went tumbling down. Turns out Daddy Chaz loved you something awful, and you took a part of him with you. So he sought revenge. It doesn't matter the many ways he tried to get it. The point is, he went after it.

I bet you're doing okay with your life. I hope you are, at least. See, I don't hold any grudges because, due to the power of writing, I can deal with it and I can grow from it. Funny thing, daddies leaving their sons. In an odd way, it makes them stronger if they channel the energy right.

Daddy Bubba has three kids now, married and committed to his kingdom. Daddy Tee is trying to make the best out of what there is out there, and Daddy Chaz found God, and God can do miracles, even with the broken and busted.

He did with me. I finally got married, despite what other men said about me. Yup, get to raise my Shuga and make a home that nobody can take from me.

My husband is a man who was made stronger by his situations, too. His daddy left, as well. His mother, too, but he had what a lot of us didn't have full time—a grandma, who was there, willing and waiting to raise and help shape him with God as his backbone. Now he wants to make sure he doesn't follow those abandonment footsteps. He says a family is a gift. I believe him.

I hope peace finds you, too, and that somewhere in your heart you think about us all, about everything, even my beautiful brown mama you once loved so well. As for me, I'm gonna keep looking for the gold at the end of the rainbow. I have a lot of living to do now that I'm older and understand people are people, blood is blood. And what makes a man is his ability to forgive, accept, and change.

My sweet Lord, if I didn't have a dream! No, this wasn't just any dream. I believe it was God speaking right to me, showing me I really closed this thing all up. At first, after I had the dream I just kept it to myself. I opened my eyes up, looked down at my daughter, and kept it to myself. My husband was at sea, so he was not there to feel me moving so early in the morning, to ask me what was going on.

But I held this dream. Then, I journaled it. I went straight upstairs and wrote it down, scene for scene. I then closed the journal up and held on to it some more. To me, it was precious, it was new. It went this way:

Me, Daddy Bubba, and Daddy Chaz had gone to church. It was late and I was the only one with a car and Daddy Chaz needed a ride home. I asked Daddy Bubba if he would go with me, and at first, he said, "No." My heart began to cry, then all of a sudden, he changed his mind. The two of them sat in the back of the mini-van and Bubba fell asleep. I tried not to look in the rearview mirror, but I knew sooner or later I would be forced to. As my eyes were fixed on the dark night sky and stars I felt a light touch on my shoulder. It was Daddy Chaz's hand. He reached toward me and said, "Sorry."

Bubba woke up and looked at him. He then said it again. He said sorry for all he ever did to hurt me. I turned forward quickly. The car was still moving, so I had to slow down. I decided to pull over to a gas station. Bubba got out and Daddy Chaz followed. This gas station had rabbits just like the one I had as a small girl. They were white with pink eyes. I loved Lillian so much, she was a good rabbit, and she always came to me in my saddest moments in that house. She'd jump up on my bed and just sit by me, quietly.

Well, as me and Bubba were in the store, Daddy Chaz decided to steal one of these rabbits. Then he took off running down the highway. Well, Bubba went after him and I started to run, then I realized I didn't steal anything. So I went back for the van and went after them.

They were walking along the highway. I pulled over and let them in. As Daddy Chaz sat down with Bubba beside him, he held this tiny bunny in his arms and said, "See Mona, I got it just for you!" He then told me again, "Mona, I am sorry, really." And he turned to look out the window.

I was silent. I petted the bunny and drove off slowly.

Bubba kept looking at me, as if I should say something, but this was not his call, it was mine, finally.

I pulled over a few miles down the highway. I could see tears coming down Daddy Chaz's face from my angle in the rearview mirror. He was human. I then reached toward his arm and as he looked at me, I told him, "I forgive you."

Amazing! This was amazing to me. Somehow in the depths of my conscious, in all my growing pains, I forgave him and the shackles were cut off my ankles, the chains torn off my heart, the bars taken away from my mind. *I was free!* This was the end of my story. All that open road, just me and my daddy brothers trying to get to Mama's for some more warm cooking after a night service at church together.

But this time God had something a little sweeter for us all. He had brought us together when we least expected it. He had made a rainbow right there in the dark! After waking up from this dream I knew nothing would ever be the same again inside me. I was rich. I was over a million dollars rich! I was debt free, and I was clean.

That dirty girl, I guess she's somewhere else now, probably in the minds of other little girls who are still trapped inside their closets. She may even be in the minds of little boys, who are confused and shook up with hurt. I know incest didn't start with me, nor did it stop with me, but I know I survived it. It took a whole lot of therapy, a lot of running and a WHOLE lot of prayer to bring me out, but I survived.

And you know, others out there can survive it, too. They can be okay and put some healing to those chambers in their minds. They don't have to be prisoners. They don't have to go on thinking it was their fault or that they have to settle with not seeing their families forever. It doesn't have to be this way, because God can take what was meant for bad and turn it into a whole lot of good. And that's the glory. See. Coming out, yelling the secrets, allowing yourself a chance. Because these chances are deserved, well deserved.

I think it matters that we know our mothers may have been hurt in their private places, or our brothers, or even our fathers. I think it matters that we recognize the power of an ugly spirit, a demonic spirit, but much more so, that we acknowledge and accept the power of a mighty God, a victorious God.

So, what does this make me? Some type of religious freak, some person who believes in the unseen world? Then, that's what I am . . . if that's what it takes for folks to recognize there is a God, and we can take hold of His strength. I know that I'm gonna be Bible-thumpin' forever because I know where I come from.

"Now, I wanna tell you I was looking for myself and trying to love myself again, and I found help with God—God is all-forgiving, and we are all somehow one, no matter what happens to us. That we can turn it around with love, 'specially love of ourselves. It was the way for me, but I don't mean to say it's the only way. We are all different. No matter who we are—Buddhist, Hindu, Muslim, Jew, or Masai warrior. That's what causes the trouble, see. People get to thinking, like that phony church cult I was in, that they have the only pipeline to God, that God speaks only through them, so they can tell people what to do, taking their life and money and self-esteem. Yeah, I'm finding my healing in God through the love teaching of the Bible. And each day is a new beginning for me to try harder, to find out who I really am.

I know the place they call the ghetto, the place where food is rare but drugs are plentiful. The place where homes stand firm on the outside, but are all broken up on the inside. It's a place where color matters, where black is black and white is unattainable. It's the place where racism roams and there is no hope for tomorrow because in the minds of the people, tomorrow may never come. They could get shot, they could overdose, they could be killed by their abuser. It's the place where secrets breed and blood is not actually thicker than water because the confusion doesn't allow it to be. It's the place where walls breathe and mamas work into the wee hours of the night trying to make ends meet while their kids try to find comfort, by any means necessary, in the depths of the night. It's the place where Narnia is real, and closets become doorways.

I know the ghetto.

The roaches in some places, the rats in others, the devil at the foot of beds. I know the ghetto and its dirty streets and what it can do to kids, to mothers, to fathers. I also know it's a frame of mind that can be turned to glory.

I know how I got to where I am, and I know in the arms of God I'll be just fine, moving into an unknown future. You see, now when I drive, the road isn't foggy, the pathway isn't crooked. I'm only a prayer away from asking God to help keep it clear and straight. I'm not saying it's like none of this ever happened and I can sit down *every* night and have tea with Daddy Chaz. No, I'm not saying that at all.

What I am saying is, it's a start. As Mama told me right up there that day in the bedroom, it's a start. All of us who have been broken and busted from our insides out, who hide pain, smother pain until it makes us sick with disease need a start, a beginning point at which to forgive. See, the mind is a tricky thing, 'cause it'll always try to play games on you. In the Christian world, they say an idle mind is the devil's workshop. I agree. But a sick, broken, unhealed mind is his playground, his carnival.

It's up to us to shut the carnival down and find the glory inside ourselves. That's what me, Shuga, and my husband do each time we take off for the weekend, watch sunsets and walk in the parks and pick up rocks. This is what we do each time we sit down to eat together, watch a movie together, or play a game. This is what we do each time we say goodnight, hug one another, kiss one another. It's inside, the glory is. Always has been.

*So now what? Sookie done said her piece. Me, I'm gonna get outta here. It sure got hot in here for a while. I think I might chase me a few rainbows, shoot, I might just call my mama. But no matter what I do, I know Sookie's gonna be all right. Ain't she something for coming on out and saying what she had to? Took a lot of guts, don'tcha think? I don't know if I could do such a thing. I'm good at things like talking and passing the torch or making an opening for someone. I'm even good at tying things together, puttin' some kind of clo-sure on 'em, but she's real good at tellin'. And you know what? She told it right, too; so right her mama won't even call her up to say, "Honey, something just ain't right, don't feel right." 'Cause Sookie's got God now, see, and He loved her just enough to give her another try at this story, from ghetto to glory. See y'all later . . . Sookie, take 'em home girl.*

I don't feel no ways tired. . . . Nobody told me the road would be easy. . . . He brought me too far to leave me this way. . . .

# Ten

I returned home. It was the holidays. The first trip was in November, the icebreaker, the Holy Spirit whispering in my heart, the devil in my ears. The one in my heart won. I returned home, with courage ready to make an ending for a beginning. That's the way God is. He doesn't keep seeing your wrongs and so I had to put on His shoes, at least give it my best. Mama always taught me to do my best. So I went with all this in mind and praying without ceasing, because you know that's where the strength comes from—praying.

My husband has been at sea for almost four months now. So listening to God required me to really lean on God's strength. I did. There was something built up inside of me, a desire not to run anymore. When Daddy Chaz came in, I had been praying silently in my heart. God heard me. The music was playing and my nephew was cracking jokes with my mama. We were all laughing and being content with our full bellies. Sweet potato pie was next.

Daddy Chaz came right in with his wife, the same woman who was beside him when he used crack, when he was in the midst of running from himself, but instead ran in a circle, then cut part of that circle open and ran into walls.

She was short, of Latin decent, cute. Her name, Evelyn. She was drug free. So was he, now. She loved this brother of mine who I myself didn't even know, at all, ever. They both came in together and Daddy Chaz yelled, "What y'all playing that worldly music for, you betta get something with the spirit of the Lord on that system there." We smiled.

As he searched Mama's music with a careful eye scan, I told him, "I have a tape."

He said, "Oh, you do?"

I then looked at him and said, "Yes."

This, I believe was the first time I ever really talked directly to him. See, I did not feel like warning my children or keeping them away. When he came in that day and demanded the spirit of the Lord be present, when he said "in the name of Jesus" in one of his sentences, my bones shuttered. It was then I realized the Holy Spirit dwelled within him. The spirit of incest was gone, back into the cement walls of that house, down in the coal room. But there was something beneath his face. But God was still shaping me, giving me strength. I decided to wait and not ask any questions, and just kept going with the moment of Thanksgiving.

We went on to play gospel charades, and he played, too. He knows the Bible, he knows the stories in it, and yes, he, too, has a passion for God. So, where did this leave me? It left me nowhere. It was time to begin. We could not start over because I honestly believe that when my brother committed those acts against me, it was not him, but something deep and ugly that was not a part of God.

I never knew my brother. He simply did not exist to me, ever. Not at any holiday gathering, if he happened to be out of prison at the time, or had been released from the many group homes that let him in, he did not exist. He was completely invisible until Thanksgiving of the year 2000. Why give the year? Why date this material when all the other stuff just comes together from the center outward, like a puzzle? Because in my heart it is important to do so. Besides, you held my hand this far during the tellin', why not go a little further on into glory?

See, glory has a few meanings, two that I know of by heart. One is that it means to go from one level to the next. The other is that it is an improvement, meaning it is good, but good can become astounding. That is the way God is and this is a God thing. Daddy Chaz stepped into our mama's house and began receiving a healing that only Jesus could perform. No amount of therapy can do what God's stripes did for us all on the cross. This year I will get him a gift, not just any gift, either. I will give him a picture of me. Why a picture? Because I am his sister. I want to make claim to that now. I would like to be on his wall, just as I would like to have him on my wall with all the other family members where he belongs, not in some back alleyway, eating from the garbage, thin, frail, breakable.

His eyes did not hold the hollowness they'd had for so many years. There was no more emptiness that I would fall into, as my insides shattered as I became little again. This matters; the eyes are the entrance to the soul. His eyes held life this time. I actually noticed they were brown.

I saw Mama looking at me at one point. It was time for him to leave and he was hugging everyone. I did not exit the room, but I stood there. I was praying, seeking God as to what I should do. The Holy Spirit said, "Wait, he will hug you and you must return it."

I stood still. Daddy Chaz reached my circumference and entered into it. He gave me a hug and told me good-bye. As I released him I saw Mama looking, checking to make sure no little girls popped out. I smiled softly, reassuring her that yes, I was okay. I am thankful that she was looking, checking, making sure. She cannot erase the past, throw it off the ends of the earth as Jesus taught us to do with our sins, but she sure is going to make sure that she always looks deep within me.

I am her daughter. Her only daughter, but that, too, is her son. What a position to be in! But there is no blame here, because evil exists. It does not care who it takes a hold of. *It simply does not care.*

The house on 19th Street is still there. On this trip home I did not return there, but I felt it tugging on me. I can lift anything up in prayer and when I crossed the state border saying, "Welcome to Washington," I lifted it up. Christmas is near and if God wanted me to go back there, I knew He would send me. But first, He put His fingertips all over me.

With my husband gone, I could easily use that as an excuse to become weak. But we are soldiers, whether together or apart. So I began to pray longer and longer and have God dress me with the armor. I had Him hold onto me in the darkest of nights when I returned home. I realized that God is stronger than my husband. As we tag-teamed and prayed about all this conclusion together, my husband in the Gulf and me on the West Coast, God put His fingertips on me.

Mama wanted to know if I was coming home for Christmas. Yes, I'll be there. I could see her smiling eyes that slant slightly upward and crease softly into her small brown cheeks, her long braids hitting her shoulders. It would be nice to grow graceful as she has, with all her heartaches and pains. It would be nice to keep standing, and to do all I can to stand and even after that still stand. I will do that. I am going home.

*Now Sookie, she done went on with this thing. See, I was going to chase a few rainbows, but now I have to turn around, see, and make sure she get all the way through this thing. Wow. So, she done saw Daddy Chaz, what a good but different thing. I thought folks like her brother were 'posed to be messed up forever. I knew he had Christ and all, but he was 'posed to be somewhere, maybe left for dead or strummin' his fingers over his lips, saying stuff over and over to himself. Wow. Sookie gettin' mighty strong now.*

*I am sorta glad I turned around to go on with this with the rest of y'all. I would've really missed something. Sookie talkin' 'bout going back home now, home-home, like back into the house on 19th Street. I am going to have to wake her at night, to make sure she stay prayed up, 'cause I know she gonna need that.*

The house started coming back to me. Stronger now. I got up one night and hit the floor. As I prayed, it became bigger. I heard His voice. I had to go back, to get physical evidence, to let God shine completely through and show His truth. But how? How would I get in? See, every time I went, no one had ever been there. No one has ever been able to live there, really. Sure, they try, they move in, but in a short time, they're gone. Some even left their things and just got out in what seemed like a hurry.

The house was always from the outside, unchanged. Yes, it was dying with time, falling apart, wooden gutters gone. But there was always no one there.

If there is one thing I learned, it is this: *God will confirm His word.* So I arose from my bedside and crawled beneath my red and blue flannel comforter. It was warm, like Mama's smile, like macaroni and cheese on a day my daddy brothers and I raced home to eat dinner after being outside all day. I fell asleep. No nightmares crept in. But God's peace remained. I was ready.

# Eleven

*Oh Lawd! Sookie done went on and got her camera and now she's off again. She on her way to "that" house to get the physical evidence of the unchanged. She started out leavin' on Saturday morning, but after prayin' and all, she took off and left Thursday night. That was kinda good though, worked in her favor. 'Cause, see, the Holy Spirit was working in her, y'all. She gonna show everyone that she was never no liar.*

This trip back for me had to be the last one, but I thought last time was going to be the last time, too, so you just never know. Remember how I said something don't rest right until I tell y'all about the house. Well, all them ghosts I've seen and the lady who helped me up from the floor when Mama wasn't home got me to thinking. It got me to thinking I am going to look up information on "that" house, see what I can find that is factual.

I wanted to know who owned it when it was built back in 1906. I wanted to know who lived there and in particular, who died there. All the dreams, all the visions, I just knew there was something beyond the surface of my torture. Me and Shuga headed to the downtown library after Mama went to work. I started by just looking up historical information on houses and houses in that area. To find the specific house on 19th Street, I'd have to go a little further.

Now, in Bible study, the pastor's wife taught us that when you are in the midst of something and you find yourself getting frustrated, that's when you should pray, asking God what exactly it is He is trying to show you. The librarian printed off some information and pointed me toward another building that held permits. This is where folks would go to find previous owners and look up what work the houses had on them in the past.

I found who owned the house back in 1922. Shuga and I then headed to another building where you could find out who paid taxes on the houses. There, they had us going through microfilm to see if we could track the owners back to 1906. This was important to me, but I was beginning to get frustrated. I heard the voice of the pastor's wife, so I prayed silently and pressed on.

As I turned over and over through this film, I began to ask myself, why? Why am I doing all this? Then a silent voice came into my heart to call my daughter back into the room. As she sat by me and I kept scrolling through, she jumped up and hit her head! She said, "I got it, Mom!" I looked at her and then she went on real fast, like if she didn't say it now it would go away forever. She told me she had seen a show about how these kids solved a murder mystery and as she spoke, it hit me, too!

As she went on and talked about tracking these people who were now dead . . . that was it! I was looking for a person! Not so much history on the house. This was spiritual and spirits dwell in people! So, where did this take us? Back down to the library.

Once in the library, we went to the desk to see if we could get help to find the obituaries on people who died in 1922. I had no idea really how to start this search. The librarian looked at me and told me it would take a *very* long time to do that. He then asked me if I had a name. I told him, yes. So we scanned through more microfilm to see if the owners I found died during that year of 1922, or even later on.

I began by finding the last name in the recording of 1945 deaths. I then kept going back until I found the exact death date of the names I had. With this, I could then look up that date in the obituary file and see if it had been printed in the daily paper and it would also tell what paper it was in. There were two papers at that time. I was focusing on *The Oregonian*.

I found the obituary index and I found the file, and *yes!* It had been printed. I was excited. I started out unsure of how to even find the information I needed. Now, the big revelation. Was this going to be the person I saw many a night, talked to, and at times couldn't talk to because my tongue was stuck in my throat?

I knew what she looked like. I described her even before I had real physical evidence. So, my daughter and I held hands and scrolled slowly through the 1947 copy of *The Oregonian*. There it was. Nellie, who lived in Oregon almost 37 years, died in her home at 4208 NE 19th Street. She was born in 1859. Her photo was printed with the obituary and my mouth fell open. It was her! I looked at Shuga and stared at this old woman who rescued me. Only God could've known I'd take the time to get proof that someone and maybe even others had died in "that" house, causing the walls to bleed and memories to stain.

As I thought about this, I was motionless in my place. Inside I was yelling, "See, Mama, I was never crazy. It was all true . . . all of it."

I remember the time Mama gave me a huge apple cider jar to put down in the cellar. It was dark in that basement and

I didn't want to go, but I couldn't tell her, "No." So, I got halfway down the steps and threw a big stick into the darkness. The stick hit the ground, rested a few moments and then it came flying back up and hit the wood I was ducking behind. I ran up them steps and hid the cider jar behind the love seat. Mama didn't find that jar for three months.

When she did I told her why I hid it, she laughed and told me it was just my daddy brothers playing tricks on me. It wasn't until almost twenty years later that she admitted it wasn't my brothers. But at that time and at that age, what could she say? I was scared to death. She saw things, too, and heard things. Many a day that lady messed up Mama's laundry, dresser drawers, and kitchen towels. So now we had it in our hands. The ghost lady that caused the walls to bleed and shake, the one Mama had no fear of.

I could hear more chambers shut in my mind. Almost done.

Her photo in the obituary was the same as I remember seeing her in the corner of my room . . . in the doorway of Daddy Chaz's room . . . at the bottom of the basement stairs. Here she was. This, to me, was confirmation of how real God is. How He will walk with you every step of the way until His work is done through you. He knew the mysteries in my mind.

I am not sure why Nellie stuck around to help me. I do know she was a member of Highland Baptist Church. I don't know if she loved the Lord or just went to church out of habit, the way some folks do, then be mean as day once they get out. I found out she had seven grandchildren and they were all girls. Maybe she just took a liking to me instead of her grave. Whatever the case may be, here I am altogether in one piece, able to tell y'all there's deliverance for those who cry in the walls.

*Look at Sookie! She had to go for a minute, but now we know for sure! That Nellie lady was real! Up and died in that house, too, leaving to roam them spirits that harmed Sookie and got into her daddy brother Chaz. There's more unrest to this Nellie lady, though, I'm sure of that. She had two sons and that house stayed in that family's hands until they was all dead and gone. But the funny thing, you don't know how any of them dies . . . and you don't know where them little grandbabies of hers is buried either. Don't ask me anything though. I'm just here for Sookie, holding her hand and all. But I think it's interesting that the same number of them little girls that Sookie rescued is the same number of that woman's grandchildren. They were all girls, too! Sookie saw 'em, too! Sometimes she'd see them with Nellie. Oh, I think I see Sookie coming back.*

That was the end for me. There was no doubt in my mind about the events that happened on 19th Street. We were prey; we were simply prey to the spirits that were there before us. But I wanted proof of how things never changed there after all those years of us being gone. I prayed that the door would be opened again and I could go in and take real photos of the inside of the house, of the tub where Nellie washed me . . .

I wanted to get a picture of the shed out back where I played, where my name still graced the door and a picture of the windows of my room where Nellie would whisper . . .

*Moan jumped out right there in front of the nice man who let Sookie and her mama in that foggy morning. They were now in Sookie's old bedroom. I tried to tell her to go back to the grave that Sookie dug, that Sookie would be okay, she could handle this, and she shook her head "no." She was in the corner of the closet, crying so deep her soul shook. Mama was trying to break through—saw Sookie strugglin' some. Sookie's tongue was tied, trying not to drown in Moan's tears. Sookie could not move. It was like someone was holding her ankles. Mama kept asking, "What is it you're seeing, Sookie?" But Moan just had her standing there, tongue on a rope an' all, and her feet in tar. She was yellin' at Sookie, tellin' her she can't leave them here in this house. She was* yellin' at Sookie to take them all back with her. Sookie said okay. She'd do anything to leave that place. Why did she go back to that house anyway? For pictures? Gosh! Now look at her. Her mama standing right in front of her, and the flash-back is just too deep. She's going back in . . .

*I see myself, Mama.*
*I'm in the closet behind*
*me. I'm crying for you,*
*Mama, it hurts. Please*
*help me, Mama, please . . .*

Somehow, Sookie then heard the Holy Spirit tellin' her to look up, look into your mama's eyes. With all that praying that was done before Sookie left Washington, death had no hold on her. Before she crossed those lines into Oregon, she had been fasting, too! She heard Him. God came straight through, uninterrupted. Oh! Those beautiful brown eyes of her mama's.

Sookie began to say, "I'm okay."

Her mama shook her head and said, "Yes, Sookie, you are okay."

Moan had gone. She took off, tears and all, even with her puddle! Man, that was a close one! But it don't matter any-way, 'cause by His stripes we are healed and Sookie is bound to have memories sometimes. It's just what happens after the memory comes that counts and from the looks of it, Sookie don't have run! as one of her options anymore. It is more like stand and let God fight, even after you have done all you can to stand, stand some more! Who'd ever thought she'd be standing up in "that" house again. What a journey this has been. And now she got all those little girls with her again. Man!

# *Epilogue*

Journeys don't end right unless you tell it just the way it was. After I had gotten what I needed so this would sit right in me, I wanted to see Daddy Chaz. Thanksgiving had been a start, but I wanted to see him again and make sure his eyes were still brown and not hollow. They were.

The doorbell rang and Daddy Chaz and his wife came on in. Mama was in her kitchen and I had been upstairs braiding Shuga's hair. Something moved in me. It was like I heard the Lord speaking to my heart. "'Shall I bring to the point of birth and then not deliver?' asks the Lord your God. 'No! Never!'"

I stopped what I was doing. Daddy Chaz was in the kitchen by the time I got down the stairs. He was crying. I almost thought that was where Moan must've run to, but what God has cleansed and made pure can't hide anymore. Daddy Chaz had been apologizing to Mama for lying and I guess all the wrong he did to me, then he tried to excuse himself and leave, but the Lord touched my heart. I went to him and told him he could not leave. He can't run anymore. He then looked at me with tears in his eyes and the words couldn't come because, how exactly do you apologize for such crimes?

He looked at Mama again for some balance. Once he got it, his eyes rested on me.

I told him, "You have to look up now, 'cause God is not a God of what?"

He said, "Shame, God is not a God of shame."

The tears kept coming and finally, after all these years, I got my silent but loud apology. God is good. As we talked, Daddy Chaz began to look taller, seeing that we were listening to him talk and love was still there. We joined hands to pray.

All of us in God's hands, with His fingertips wrapped around us, speaking tongues, saying Amen! Once we were done, Mama and Daddy Chaz's wife hugged, and then he and I hugged. I felt his heart right through his shirt. I looked him in the eyes and told him, "I'm looking forward to getting to know you, big brother, it's been a long time." As he looked at me and our eyes made contact for the first time in our life,

I heard the gates of hell shut up, I heard the screaming of demons that have tried to divide families for centuries, I heard their nails scrape the black hot walls in defeat.

Angels were dancing. Glory was shining down on us all . . . for now.

*"But our families will continue; generation after generation will be preserved by Your protection."*

PSALM 102:28